Treasures

INTERACTIVE
Read-Aloud
ANTHOLOGY with PLAYS

Grade 1

Macmillan
McGraw-Hill

ACKNOWLEDGMENTS

BEVERLY BILLINGSLY BORROWS A BOOK by Alexander Stadler. Copyright © 2002 by Alexander Stadler. Used by permission of Harcourt, Inc.

THE TOWN MOUSE AND THE COUNTRY MOUSE retold by Lorinda Bryan Cauley. Copyright © 1984 by Lorinda Bryan Cauley. Used by permission of G. P. Putnam's Sons.

"Just Watch" by Myra Cohn Livingston, from READ-ALOUD RHYMES FOR THE VERY YOUNG. Copyright © 1985 by Myra Cohn Livingston. Used by permission of Marian Reiner.

"The Tortoise and the Hare" from ONCE UPON A BEDTIME STORY retold by Jane Yolen. Copyright © 1997 by Jane Yolen. Used by permission of Boyds Mills Press, Inc.

"Growing Old" by Rose Henderson, from THE RANDOM HOUSE BOOK OF POETRY FOR CHILDREN. Copyright © 1983 by Random House, Inc. Used by permission of Random House, Inc.

"I'm Growing Up!" by Mariana Relos, from *Current Health 1*, Oct. 2002, Vol. 26 Issue 2. Copyright © 2002 by Weekly Reader Corporation. Used by permission of Weekly Reader Corporation.

"Snake on the Loose!" by Gibbs Davis, from "Animal House" in *Storyworks*, Feb./Mar. 2001, Vol. 8 Issue 5. Copyright © 2001 by Scholastic Inc. Used by permission of Scholastic Inc.

"The Three Billy Goats Gruff" adapted by Carolyn Quattrocki from TREASURY OF BEDTIME STORIES adapted by Jane Jerrard, Bette Killion, Carolyn Quattrocki. Copyright © 1998 by Publications International, Ltd. Used by permission of Publications International, Ltd.

UP, UP, UP! IT'S APPLE-PICKING TIME by Jody Fickes Shapiro. Copyright © 2003 by Jody Fickes Shapiro. Used by permission of Holiday House.

"Goldilocks and the Three Bears" adapted by Jane Jerrard from TREASURY OF BEDTIME STORIES adapted by Jane Jerrard, Bette Killion, Carolyn Quattrocki. Copyright © 1998 by Publications International, Ltd. Used by permission of Publications International, Ltd.

MAKE WAY FOR DUCKLINGS by Robert McCloskey. Copyright © 1941 by The Viking Press. Used by permission of Viking Penguin Inc.

JOHNNY APPLESEED by Patricia Demuth. Copyright © 1996 by Patricia Demuth. Used by permission of Grosset & Dunlap, a division of Penguin Putnam Books for Young Readers.

WE'RE GOING ON A BEAR HUNT by Michael Rosen. Copyright © 1989 by Michael Rosen. Used by permission of Scholastic Inc.

"Habitats: Where Animals Live" from WORLD ALMANAC FOR KIDS, 2004. Copyright © 2004 by World Almanac Education Group, Inc. Used by permission of World Almanac Education Group, Inc.

Continued on page 281

A

The McGraw·Hill Companies

Macmillan McGraw-Hill

CONTENTS

Unit 3

Unit 4

Unit 5

Unit 6

Plays and Choral Readings

INTERACTIVE
Read-Aloud
ANTHOLOGY with PLAYS

~ Developing Listening Comprehension ~

Read Alouds help to build children's listening comprehension. This anthology offers selections from a variety of genres, including biography, fiction, folk tales, nonfiction, songs, and poetry, to share with children. Instruction is provided with each selection to develop specific **comprehension strategies.** Children are asked to **set a purpose for listening,** as well as to **determine the author's purpose** for writing. Using the instruction provided, each Read Aloud becomes an enjoyable, purposeful learning experience.

~ What Makes a Read Aloud Interactive? ~

With each selection, **Teacher Think Alouds** are provided to help you model the use of comprehension strategies during reading. Using Think Alouds allows children to listen and to observe how a good reader uses strategies to get meaning from text. After reading, children are given the opportunity to apply the comprehension strategy. Children are asked to "think aloud" as they apply the strategy. By listening to a **Student Think Aloud** you can determine if the child is applying the comprehension strategy appropriately and with understanding.

Think-Aloud Copying Masters included in the Read-Aloud Anthology provide sentence starters to help children "think aloud" about a strategy.

Plays and Choral Reading

Reader's Theater for Building Fluency

You can use the plays and choral reading found at the back of this anthology to perform a Reader's Theater with children. Reading fluency is developed by repeated practice in reading text, especially when the reading is done orally. Reader's Theater can help build children's fluency skills because it engages them in a highly motivating activity that provides an opportunity to read—and reread—text orally. As children practice their assigned sections of the "script," they have multiple opportunities to increase their accuracy in word recognition and their rate of reading. Children are also strongly motivated to practice reading with appropriate phrasing and expression.

Performing Reader's Theater

• Assign speaking roles.

• Do not always assign the speaking role with the most text to the most fluent reader. Readers who need practice reading need ample opportunity to read.

• Have children rehearse by reading and rereading their lines over several days. In these rehearsals, allow time for teacher and peer feedback about pace, phrasing, and expression.

• Children do not memorize their lines, but rather read their lines from the script.

• No sets, costumes, or props are necessary.

Beverly Billingsly Borrows a Book

a fantasy

by Alexander Stadler

Genre: Fantasy

Comprehension Strategy: Story Structure

Think-Aloud Copying Master number 1

Before Reading

Genre: Explain to children that a fantasy is a story that has characters, settings and events that could be true or make-believe. In the story they will hear, Beverly Billingsly is a little mouse who acts like a real person.

Expand Vocabulary: Before reading aloud the story, introduce the following vocabulary words to children.

> *shelving: putting on a shelf*
>
> *single:* one
>
> *overdue:* late; past a deadline

Set a Purpose for Reading: Suggest that children listen to the story to learn about Beverly's problem and how she goes about solving it.

During Reading

Use the Think Alouds during the first reading of the story. Notes about the genre may be used during subsequent readings.

Beverly Billingsly Borrows a Book

by Alexander Stadler

Every Tuesday afternoon, Beverly Billingsly went to the library with her mother. Beverly loved the library. And this Tuesday would be even more special than usual.

"Is today the day I get my own card?" Beverly asked.

"Yes," answered her mother.

Mrs. Del Rubio was the new librarian.

Beverly straightened her bow and said, "I would like a library card, please."

"Wonderful," said Mrs. Del Rubio, as she finished <u>shelving</u> some books. "Please follow me to my desk."

Mrs. Del Rubio had a long list of questions. Beverly answered each one correctly. Her mother didn't have to help her with a <u>single</u> thing.

A few seconds later, Mrs. Del Rubio looked Beverly straight in the eye and said, "Miss Billingsly, you are now a member of the Piedmont Public Library. You may take out any book you like."[1]

Beverly searched the shelves until she found what she wanted—a big shiny book called *Dinosaurs of the Cretaceous Period*.

As Mrs. Del Rubio stamped the book, she said, "Remember to return it by April seventh."

Beverly loved *Dinosaurs of the Cretaceous Period*. She couldn't put it down. On Wednesday, after school, she studied the iguanodon. On Thursday and Friday, she read about the ankylosaurus.

She spent several days building a prehistoric jungle habitat.

Beverly read everywhere—at the dinner table, in bed, even in the tub.

On Monday morning, Beverly woke up early to finish the final chapter, "Eating Habits of the Triceratops."

As she turned the last page, she saw, stamped inside the back cover: RETURN BY APRIL 7.

Beverly looked at her calendar. The date was April eighth.

"Oh no," she whispered. "I'll return it today after school," she told herself.

At lunch, Beverly sat next to Sheila Rose Hoffstetter. "Do you know what happens when a person is late returning a library book?" Beverly asked.

"I'm not sure," Sheila said, "but I think you have to pay a lot of money."

"Like how much?" asked Beverly.

"Oh, like a thousand dollars, I think," answered Sheila.

Carlton Chlomsky had been listening to their conversation. "My mother's friend's cousin's brother was late with a library book, and he went to jail," Carlton said.

"I can't believe it!" said Beverly.

"Believe it," said Carlton, munching on a carrot.

That afternoon, as she was walking toward the library, Beverly's stomach started to ache. "Maybe I'll return the book tomorrow," she said to herself in a small voice.[2]

Beverly didn't eat much at dinner. "I'm not hungry," she told her parents.

"Even with chocolate cake for dessert?" asked her mother.

"Is anything wrong?" asked her father.

Beverly shook her head and went to bed.

That night, Beverly had a strange and frightening dream. A big green triceratops stuck its head through her window.

"Return meeeee!" it growled. "Return me, Beverleeeeeee! I am overduuuuuuuuuuue! Return me or I will gobble you up!"

"But you're an herbivore!" Beverly shouted. "You eat only small plants and other vegetation! It says so on pages forty-two and forty-three!"

Suddenly Beverly woke up. Her mother was sitting on the edge of her bed.

"What's the matter, Beverly?" her mother asked.

"I have to return the book, and the dinosaur is mad at me, and Mrs. Del Rubio is going to take all my money, and I don't want to go to jail!"

Mrs. Billingsly smoothed the fur on Beverly's ears and gave her shoulder a little squeeze.

"Don't worry, honey," she said. "Nobody ever went to jail for an overdue library book. Tomorrow we'll go and return the book together."

The next day, after school, Beverly and her mother went to the library.

Beverly took a deep breath as she walked up to Mrs. Del Rubio's desk. "My book is overdue," she said.

Mrs. Del Rubio opened the book to the back. "Well, it's only a couple of days late, dear," she said. "We won't worry about it.

Think Aloud

[2]Beverly is worried about her library book. Her friends make her worry even more. I wonder what Beverly will do next.

Genre Study

Fantasy In a real story, the animals would act like animals. In this make-believe story, Beverly and the other mice act like people.

Just try to be more careful next time." And then she closed the book and smiled.[3]

"Now isn't that funny?" said Mrs. Del Rubio. "Oliver Shumacher walked in here not five minutes ago and asked about this very book. I think he's in your grade. Shall we take it to him?"

"Hi," said Oliver.

"Hello," said Beverly. "What are you working on?"

"I'm doing a report on pterodactyls," said Oliver.

"Did you know there was one that had a fifty-foot wingspan?" asked Beverly.

"And it could still fly?!" asked Oliver.

"Yes," said Beverly. "Here, I'll show you. There's a picture of one in chapter eleven."

And that is how the Piedmont Dinosaur Club began.

After Reading

Retell the Story: Invite children to draw a picture of Beverly (the mouse) during one part of the story. Then have them share their drawings and tell what Beverly is thinking about.

Use the Copying Master on page 1 to prompt children to share a question they had about the story.

"I wonder . . ."

Think and Respond

1. What words would you use to describe Beverly? *Possible responses: responsible, careful, worried* **Inferential**

2. How can you tell that this story is a fantasy? *Possible response: The story combines make-believe things with things that could really happen. Visits to libraries are very real, but mice don't act as people do.* **Genre**

3. What do you think the author wanted you to learn from this story? *Possible response: Sometimes a problem is not as big and scary as you first think it is.* **Author's Purpose**

The Town Mouse and the Country Mouse

an Aesop fable

retold by Lorinda Bryan Cauley

Genre: Fable

Comprehension Strategy: Story Structure

Think-Aloud Copying Master number 6

Before Reading

Genre: Tell children that a fable is a short story that teaches a lesson. Explain that the characters in a fable are usually animals that talk.

Expand Vocabulary: Introduce the following words before reading this fable:

> *imagine:* to make up a picture in your mind

> *curiosity:* a strong feeling of wanting to know or learn

> *luxury:* something that gives great comfort and pleasure

> *hectic:* full of confusion or excitement

Set a Purpose for Reading: Have children listen to find out what happens when a country mouse visits a town mouse.

During Reading

Use the Think Alouds during the first reading of the story. Notes about the genre and cultural perspective may be used during subsequent readings.

The Town Mouse and the Country Mouse

an Aesop fable

retold by Lorinda Bryan Cauley

The Country Mouse lived by himself in a snug little hole in an old log in a field of wildflowers.

One day he decided to invite his cousin the Town Mouse for a visit, and he sent him a letter.

When his cousin arrived, the Country Mouse could hardly wait to show him around. They went for a walk, and on the way they gathered a basket of acorns.

They picked some wild wheat stalks.

They stopped by the river and sat on the bank, cooling their feet.

And on the way home for supper, they picked some wildflowers for the house.

The Country Mouse settled his cousin in an easy chair with a cup of fresh mint tea and then went about preparing the best country supper he had to offer.

He made a delicious soup of barley and corn.

He simmered a root stew seasoned with thyme.

Then he made a rich nutcake for dessert, which he would serve hot from the oven.

The Town Mouse watched in amazement. He had never seen anyone work so hard.

But when they sat down to eat, the Town Mouse only picked and nibbled at the food on his plate. Finally, turning up his long nose, he said, "I cannot understand, Cousin, how you can work so hard and put up with food such as this. Why, you live no better than the ants and work twice as hard."[1]

"It may be simple food," said the Country Mouse, "but there is plenty of it. And there is nothing I enjoy more than gathering everything fresh from the fields and cooking a hot supper."

"I should die of boredom," the Town Mouse complained. "I never have to work for my supper, and in my life there is hardly ever a dull moment."

Genre Study

Fable: A fable is a short story that teaches a lesson. The characters are usually talking animals. For example, the Town Mouse and the Country Mouse behave like people. They talk to one another and have feelings and opinions. In this story, the Town Mouse and the Country Mouse have different opinions.

Think Aloud

[1] The Town Mouse thinks his cousin works too hard for food. He does not like the food in the country either. I get the feeling the Town Mouse does not like the country.

"I can't <u>imagine</u> any other life," answered the Country Mouse.

"In that case, dear Cousin, come back to town with me and see what you have been missing."

So, out of <u>curiosity</u>, the Country Mouse agreed to go. Off they went, scampering across fields while avoiding the cows and down a dirt lane, edged with bright flowers, until at last they reached the cobblestones leading into town.

The streetlights flickered eerily, and with each horse and carriage that clip-clopped by, the Country Mouse trembled with fear.

At last they reached a row of elegant town houses, their windows glowing in lamplight. "This is where I live," said the Town Mouse. The Country Mouse had to admit that it looked warm and inviting.

They went inside and crept past the tick-tock of the grandfather clock in the hall and into the living room. The Town Mouse led his cousin to a small entrance hole behind the wood basket next to the fireplace.

Once inside, the Town Mouse lit a candle and started a fire. The Country Mouse looked around the room. It was so much grander than his little hole in the old log. Why, his cousin's bed was covered with a fine silk handkerchief as a bedspread.

They had been traveling all day, and the Country Mouse was tired and hungry. So he was surprised when his cousin started to go back through the entrance hole. "Could we have something to eat before you show me around?" he asked timidly.

"But of course," said his cousin. "That is where we are going. To have a feast of a supper."

They went through the living room and into the dining room and there on a large table was the remains of a fine supper. The Country Mouse's eyes were wide with astonishment. He had never seen so much food all at once, nor so many kinds.

"Help yourself," invited the Town Mouse. "Whatever you like is yours for the taking."

The Country Mouse scampered across the starched white linen and stared at the dishes. Creamy puddings, cheeses, biscuits, and chocolate candies. Cakes, jellies, fresh fruit, and nuts![2]

It all looked and smelled delicious. He hardly knew where to begin.

Think Aloud

[2] I thought the author's description was important in this story because she did a good job of helping me picture how fancy the town house is and how much food there is to eat there.

He took a sip from a tall, sparkling glass and thought, "This is heaven. Maybe I have been wrong to have wasted my life in the country."

He had just started nibbling on a piece of strawberry cake when suddenly the dining room doors flew open and two servants came in to clear away the dishes.

The two mice scampered off the table and hid beneath it. When they heard the doors close again, the Town Mouse coaxed his cousin back onto the table to eat what was left.

But they had hardly taken two bites when the doors opened again and a small girl in her nightdress ran in to look for her doll, which had fallen under the table. This time the Town Mouse hid behind the jug of cream and the Country Mouse crouched in terror behind the butter dish. But she didn't see them.

As soon as the girl was gone, the Town Mouse began to eat again. But the Country Mouse stood listening. "Come on," said his cousin. "Relax and enjoy this delicious cheese."

But before the Country Mouse could even taste it, he heard barking and growling outside the door. "Wha-, what's that?" he stammered.[3]

"It is only the dogs of the house," answered the Town Mouse. "Don't worry. They're not allowed in the dining room." And with that, the doors burst open and in bounded two roaring dogs. This time the mice scampered down the side of the table, out of the room, and back to the hole in the living room just in the nick of time.

"Cousin, you may live in <u>luxury</u> here, but I'd rather eat my simple supper in the country than a feast like this in fear for my life. I'm going home right away," said the Country Mouse.

"Yes, I suppose that the <u>hectic</u> life of the town is not for everybody, but it's what makes me happy. If you ever need a little excitement in your life, you can come for another visit," replied his cousin.

"And any time you want a little peace and quiet and healthy food, come and visit me in the country," said the Country Mouse.

Then off he went to his snug little home in the fields, whistling a tune and looking forward to a good book by the fire and a mug of hot barley-corn soup.

Think Aloud

[3] At first I thought the Country Mouse was going to like living in the town, but after all these scary things happening to him, I think the Country Mouse doesn't like it at all.

After Reading

Retell the Story: Help children make simple finger puppets of the Country Mouse and the Town Mouse. Have them retell the story with a partner using their finger puppets.

Student Think Aloud

Use Copying Master number 6 to prompt children to share what parts of the story helped them understand the difference between Country Mouse and City Mouse's lives.

"I thought _____ was important in this story because . . ."

Cultural Perspective

Aesop's fables came from Greece more than two thousand years ago. No one is sure whether or not the author Aesop truly existed.

Think and Respond

1. Who are you more like—the Country Mouse or the Town Mouse? Why? *Responses will vary.* **Analytical**

2. Most fables have animals that act as people do. How are the animals in this fable like people? *Possible response: The mice speak and act as people do. They have feelings just as people do, too.* **Genre**

3. What does the author want you to learn from this fable? *Possible responses: There's no place like home. Different people like different things.* **Author's Purpose**

Just Watch

a poem

by Myra Cohn Livingston

Genre: Poetry

Poetic Element: Rhyming Words, Repetition

Comprehension Strategy: Generate Questions

Think-Aloud Copying Master number 1

Before Reading

Genre: Explain to children that a rhyming poem contains words that sound alike. Rhyming words may appear at the end of each line or, as in this poem, at the end of every other stanza, a group of sentences. This particular poem also contains words that are repeated. Writers repeat words to create a rhythm in the poem.

Expand Vocabulary: To help children understand the poem, introduce this word before reading:

watch: look

Set a Purpose for Reading: Have children listen for the poem's rhyming words and rhythm.

During Reading

Read through the poem the first time without interruptions. Then reread, drawing children's attention to the Think Aloud and the genre note.

Just Watch

by Myra Cohn Livingston

Watch

  how high

  I'm jumping.

Watch

  how far

  I hop,

Watch

  how long

  I'm skipping,

Watch

  how fast

  I stop![1]

After Reading

Retell: Have children retell the poem by acting out the words.

Student Think Aloud

Use Copying Master number 1 to prompt children to share any questions they had about the poem.

"I wonder . . ."

Think and Respond

1. To whom do you think the person in this poem is speaking? Why? *Possible response: It might be a mother or father because I am always asking my parents to watch me do things.* **Critical**

2. What makes this poem fun to hear? *Possible response: The rhythm and rhyming words; the bouncy action words* **Genre**

3. What do you think is the poet's purpose for writing this poem? *Possible response: She wanted to entertain the reader with words and actions that children say and do everyday.* **Author's Purpose**

The Tortoise and the Hare

an Aesop fable

retold by Jane Yolen

Genre: Fable

Comprehension Strategy: Story Structure

Think-Aloud Copying Master number 3

Before Reading

Genre: Remind children that a fable is a short story that teaches a moral, or lesson. Ask children to retell the lesson they learned in the previous fable they heard, "The Town Mouse and the Country Mouse."

Expand Vocabulary: Introduce the following words before reading this fable:

> *hare:* an animal that is related to a rabbit
>
> *boasted:* bragged
>
> *tortoise:* a land turtle
>
> *laggard:* someone who moves very slowly

Set a Purpose for Reading: Have children listen to find out what lesson Hare learns from Tortoise.

During Reading

Use the Think Alouds during the first reading of the story. Notes about the genre and cultural perspective may be used during subsequent readings.

The Tortoise and the Hare

an Aesop Fable
retold by Jane Yolen

Once upon a time there was a <u>hare</u> who was proud of his speed. "I am the fastest runner in the land," he <u>boasted</u> to every creature he met.

In fact he boasted so much that the rest of the animals soon got tired of listening to him. But only one, the <u>tortoise</u>, decided to do anything about it.

"If you are so fast," Tortoise said, "prove it."

"What—against you?" Hare laughed. "You are the forest slowpoke. You are a <u>laggard</u> and a lugabout, a dawdler and a slug. I will have no problem beating you."[1]

"Fast talk," retorted Tortoise, "is not fast walk."

"Name the place, lie-abed," Hare said.

So they fixed a time and place for a race and went their separate ways, Hare to his local diner where he laughed with his few friends, and Tortoise to practice running.

The day of the race was sunny. Frog had the starter gun and when it rang out, the race was begun.

Hare went galloping around the first bend, and when he saw that Tortoise had barely left the starting gate, he got a silly grin on his face.[2]

"Tortoise is such a plodder, I will have time for a nap and will still lap him." So Hare lay down for a bit and was soon fast asleep.

Tortoise was a plodder indeed. But he put one foot steadily in front of another. When he came around the bend and saw Hare asleep, he tiptoed past. "You sleep and I'll slip by," he whispered, and he did just that.

The sun and Tortoise kept pace, and just at dusk Hare awoke. He looked behind him. No Tortoise.

Think Aloud

[1] *The author has Hare use* laggard, lugabout, dawdler, *and* slug *to describe Tortoise. I think these words tell me that Tortoise is very slow.*

Think Aloud

[2] *I was able to picture in my mind Hare starting out very fast and galloping down the road. And I can imagine the look on his face when he saw Tortoise so far behind.*

Genre Study

Fable: Many fables do not include the lesson in the fable. This fable is different. It states the lesson at the end of the story.

He looked ahead—Tortoise! Tortoise was just about to cross the finish line.[3]

Hare ran as fast as he could, which was very fast indeed. But he could not run fast enough. Tortoise crossed the finish line first and won the race.

"Slow and steady is the pace, slow and steady wins the race," said Tortoise.

All the other forest animals picked up that line and sang it long into the night.

And Hare went home, never to boast of his speed again.

After Reading

Retell the Story: Have children draw three pictures to show the beginning, middle, and end of the story. Have them use their pictures to retell the story.

Student Think Aloud

Use Copying Master number 3 to prompt children to tell what they were able to visualize as they listened to the story.

"I was able to picture in my mind . . ."

Cultural Perspective

Many cultures around the world tell stories about tortoises and turtles. Some Native American cultures tell about a giant sea turtle that rose from the ocean and sprouted plants on its back. In these stories, the turtle's shell becomes Earth.

Think and Respond

1. Were you surprised that Tortoise won the race? Why? *Possible response: Yes, because tortoises move so slowly and hares hop so fast.* **Critical**

2. What are some clues that tell you this story is a fable? *Possible responses: There are talking animals; the story teaches a lesson.* **Genre**

3. What lesson does the author want you to learn from the fable? Slow and steady wins the race. What do you think that means? *Possible response: Be patient and stay focused on your goal.* **Author's Purpose**

Growing Old

a poem

by Rose Henderson

Genre: Poetry

Poetic Element: Rhyme

Comprehension Strategy: Visualize

Think-Aloud Copying Master number 3

Before Reading

Genre: This rhyming poem has words that rhyme at the end of each pair of lines. The poet also uses describing words to help readers form a picture as they read.

Expand Vocabulary: To help children understand the poem, introduce these words before reading:

> *cunning:* pleasing, likable
>
> *piles:* a lot of something thrown together
>
> *ripples:* little waves

Set a Purpose for Reading: Have children listen for details that will help them imagine what Grandma Lee looks like.

During Reading

Read through the poem the first time without interruptions. Then reread, drawing children's attention to the Think Aloud and the genre note.

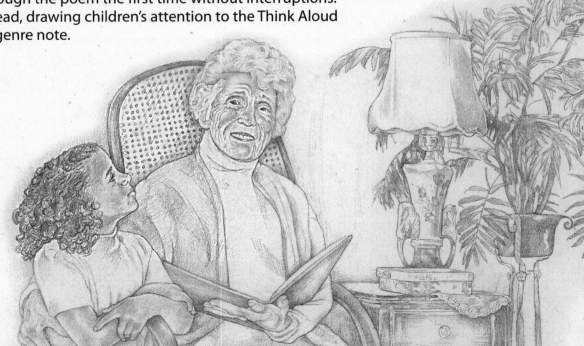

Growing Old

by Rose Henderson

When I grow old I hope to be
As beautiful as Grandma Lee.
Her hair is soft and fluffy white.
Her eyes are blue and candle bright.[1]
And down her cheeks are <u>cunning</u> <u>piles</u>
Of little <u>ripples</u> when she smiles.

Think Aloud

[1] *I was able to picture in my mind how Grandma Lee's eyes looked.*

Genre Study

Poem: The poet wants the reader to picture Grandma Lee's wrinkles as ripples, or small waves of water.

After Reading

Retell: Have children draw a picture of Grandma Lee. Have them describe their pictures.

Student Think Aloud

Use the Copying Master number 3 to prompt children to share what the poem made them picture in their minds.

"I was able to picture in my mind . . ."

Think and Respond

1. What kind of a person do you think Grandma Lee is? Why? *Possible response: She is happy and kind because she smiles and her eyes are bright.* **Critical**

2. The poet states that Grandma Lee's eyes are bright like a candle. What could you compare her blue eyes to so readers could picture the color? *Possible responses: the sky, an ocean, a sapphire* **Visualize**

3. How do you think the author feels about growing old? *Possible response: Growing old can be beautiful.* **Author's Purpose**

I'm Growing Up!

by Mariana Relos

Genre: Nonfiction

Text Structure: Cause/Effect

Comprehension Strategy: Text Structure

Think-Aloud Copying Master number 1

Before Reading

Genre: Explain to children that you will be reading a text about growing up. The story gives information about how their bodies grow.

Expand Vocabulary: To help children understand the informational text, introduce the following words and terms:

    shrink: get smaller

    muscles: parts of the body that help it move

    variety: many different types of something

    growth spurt: a period when the body grows quickly

Set a Purpose for Reading: Ask children to listen for healthy things they can do to help their bodies grow.

During Reading

Use the Think Alouds during the first reading of the text. The genre note may be used during subsequent readings.

I'm Growing Up!

by Mariana Relos

Laura could bet her whole allowance on it. Those pants fit her perfectly the last time she wore them. But now they're too short! How did the pants <u>shrink</u>? The truth is that Laura's pants did not shrink; she grew!

Laura has been *growing up* since she was inside her mother's womb. And she won't stop *growing* until she is about 15 years old. Her brother, George, will grow until he is about 17 years old.

During all those growing years, Laura's and George's bones will get longer, thicker, and harder. Their <u>muscles</u> will get bigger. From head to toe, their bodies will increase in size and weight. And so will all the organs inside their bodies.

Laura is surprised. How can all this growing up happen and she not be aware of it? Laura doesn't notice her body growing day by day because people grow very slowly. People grow slower than most other animals do. Laura realizes how slowly she grows when she compares her growth to that of her dog, Tex. Tex grew from being a puppy to an adult dog in just two years![1]

Sometimes Laura and George wonder if they will be taller than, shorter than, or the same height as their parents. As a rule, tall parents have tall children, and short parents tend to have short children. This is because parents pass on to their children genes that determine how much they will grow.

There is more than one gene affecting height. One of these genes is the growth hormone gene. Growth hormone is a chemical produced by the pituitary (pih-TOO-ih-tare-ree) gland, and the blood carries it throughout the body. This hormone makes Laura's and George's bones grow. Without it, a child would remain small. Genes are very important factors that affect growth, but they are not the only factors.

One of the other factors that affects Laura's growth is nutrition. Laura's body uses the proteins, carbohydrates, and fats in food to build new bone, muscle, and other body organs and tissues.

Think Aloud

[1] *I notice the author asks a question about why Laura is not aware that she is growing. I wondered about that, too. I read on to find out that the author answers this question. She says that Laura grows very slowly every day.*

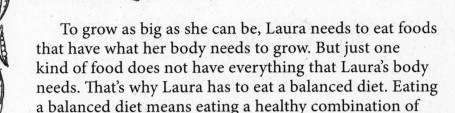

Think Aloud

[2] *I wonder what kinds of foods are considered carbohydrates, proteins, and fats. I will read ahead to find out. However, if I don't find the information in this text, I may have to look in another source to figure out what the author means.*

Genre Study

Nonfiction: Many nonfiction stories provide information. Here, the writer gives specific examples of foods that have the mineral calcium in them. These details are helpful.

Think Aloud

[3] *I wonder how the doctor can tell whether a person's growth is normal or not. I will read on to find out.*

To grow as big as she can be, Laura needs to eat foods that have what her body needs to grow. But just one kind of food does not have everything that Laura's body needs. That's why Laura has to eat a balanced diet. Eating a balanced diet means eating a healthy combination of carbohydrates, proteins, and fats every day.[2]

Laura's body also needs minerals and vitamins. To build healthy new bone, her body uses large amounts of the mineral calcium. Three cups of milk a day will give Laura the calcium she needs. Other dairy products and some fruits and vegetables provide calcium too. Eating a <u>variety</u> of fruits and vegetables can give Laura the vitamins she needs for growth.

But eating a balanced diet is not enough. Another factor that affects Laura's growth is exercise. Laura knows that if she spends most of her free time doing her favorite exercises, like riding her bike or playing a sport, she will help her body grow strong bones. But if she sits down to watch TV or play computer games most of the time, her bones won't grow as strong.

Some diseases may slow down Laura's growth. During some seasons, Laura has trouble breathing, especially when she exercises hard. The doctor said she has mild asthma and prescribed medication to control it.

The doctor explained that she must take her medication or her asthma may get worse. If asthma is severe for years without medication, it may make Laura very sick, and this could slow down her growth. But if Laura controls her asthma with medication, it won't affect her growth.

What is normal growth? Most kids grow normally. Even those who are taller or shorter than the majority of kids usually have a normal growth pattern. One year ago, George was the shortest in his class, but now he's as tall as most of his classmates.

This happens because kids of the same age grow at different rates. Some grow quickly; others catch up on their growth later. During the time when George was the shortest in his class, he went to the doctor to see if being the shortest was normal.[3]

The doctor compared George's height with a growth chart. George's height was normal for his age, just on the "small size" side of the chart.

But like most kids, when George started his teen years, he had a <u>growth spurt</u>. He ended up being almost as tall as most of his friends. At first, George didn't like being shorter than some of his friends. But in time he realized that his height was normal for him. It had nothing to do with George's ability to do well in school, or in sports, or in making friends. George is still taller than Laura, though. And this gives them something to joke about!

After Reading

Retell the Story: Ask children to retell facts that they learned about growing up in this text. List the facts on the board and have children help you number them inthe order in which they are presented in the article.

Student Think Aloud

Use Copying Master number 1 to prompt children to share a question they have about how their bodies grow.

"I wonder . . ."

Think and Respond

1. What was the most important thing you learned about growing up? *Responses will vary.* **Analytical**

2. The story gives many examples of things that can affect a person's growth. Choose one and tell what effect it has on a person's growth. *Possible responses: Illness might slow a person's growth; exercising helps a person grow strong bones.* **Text Structure**

3. Why do you think Mariana Relos wrote this story? *Possible response: She wanted people to learn about how their bodies grow.* **Author's Purpose**

ANiMaL HOUSE

by Gibbs Davis

~~~~~~~~~~~~~~~~~~~~~~~~~~~~~~~~

Genre: Nonfiction

Comprehension Strategy: Text Structure

Think-Aloud Copying Master number 7

 ### Before Reading

Genre: Explain to children that nonfiction books or articles tell about things that are real. Nonfiction authors often give details and examples to help us understand the topic.

Expand Vocabulary: Introduce the following words before reading to help children understand the text:

> *average:* normal
>
> *exotic:* wild
>
> *reptilian:* like a reptile
>
> *chaos:* confusion

Set a Purpose for Reading: Have children listen to find out what kinds of pets have lived in the White House.

 ### During Reading

Use the Think Alouds during the first reading of the text. Notes about the genre and cultural perspective may be used during subsequent readings.

ANIMAL HOUSE

by Gibbs Davis

For the <u>average</u> family, a pet means a dog or a cat. But the President of the United States and his family are hardly average. And neither are their pets. The President's pets get to live in the most famous house in the country. The White House has 132 rooms. That's some doghouse!

Sometimes the President receives <u>exotic</u> four-footed gifts from foreign officials. Zebras, lion cubs, and baby hippos are shipped to the nearest zoo. However, some equally wild pets, such as bears, raccoons, and even alligators, have remained in the White House to live with the First Family.

Theodore Roosevelt led our country during a time of great change (1901 to 1909). Inventions like the Model T car and the Wright Brothers' powered airplane were transforming American lives. Theodore Roosevelt was the first President to fly in an airplane, ride in a car, and submerge in a submarine. But this robust President never lost his love of nature. Roosevelt worked to conserve millions of acres of wilderness. The Teddy Bear was even named after him.

His daughter Alice was the most famous teenager in the country. Bright and high-spirited, Alice caught the nation's imagination—and she loved it. There were almost as many newspaper articles about young Alice as there were about her father!

A girl like Alice couldn't have just any ordinary pet. She decided on a pet garter snake. She named it Emily Spinach because it was as green as spinach and as thin as her Aunt Emily.

Alice was invited to many elegant parties. Emily Spinach was not. But Alice wouldn't consider excluding her <u>reptilian</u> friend. Alice dressed up for the party, dropped her slender pet into her purse, and snapped it shut.

At the party, Alice waited for a quiet moment and cracked open her purse. Emily slithered out. The President's daughter laughed as she watched the ladies race for the door, screaming.[1]

Emily wasn't the only Roosevelt who liked snakes. Her brother Quentin bought four snakes from a local pet shop and brought them home to show his father. The President was in the Oval Office holding an important meeting when Quentin barged in with his bag of snakes.

When Quentin dropped them on a table so that he could hug his father, there was instant <u>chaos</u> in the room! The five-foot king

Genre Study

Nonfiction:
Nonfiction books give information about real things. The author uses facts to explain something which makes the topic more interesting.

Think Aloud

[1] *I noticed the author used facts about real White House pets. These facts help me understand how exciting and often funny having a pet in the White House can be.*

snake attacked the grass snake, while the black snake did battle with the gold-banded snake. The senators scrambled for safety while the snakes fought and slithered off. Eventually, Roosevelt and his son tracked down the escaped reptiles and they were returned to the pet shop.

Nothing could separate the six Roosevelt children from their beloved pets. When Archie Roosevelt was sick in bed with the measles, his brothers knew just how to cheer him up. They sneaked his calico pony, Algonquin, into the White House elevator and took him upstairs to Archie's bedroom![2]

Think Aloud

[2] *This story is mostly about animals that have lived in the White House.*

After Reading

Retell: Invite children to draw a picture that shows what happened to one of the pets that lived in the White House. Have them tell about their pictures.

Student Think Aloud

Use Copying Master number 7 to prompt children to summarize their favorite part of the selection.

Cultural Perspective

Leaders of other countries often gave animals to the President as gifts. The King of Siam gave President James Buchanan a herd of elephants!

"This story is mostly about . . ."

Think and Respond

1. Do you think snakes were good pets to have in the White House? Why or why not? *Possible response: No, because many people are afraid of snakes.* **Inferential**

2. What makes this nonfiction selection interesting to read? *Possible response: The author includes funny stories about White House pets.* **Genre**

3. Why do you think the author wrote this selection? *Possible response: The author wants us to know about some of the pets that have lived in the White House.* **Author's Purpose**

Mary Had a Little Lamb

a nursery rhyme

by Sarah Josepha Hale

Genre: Nursery Rhyme
Poetic Element: Rhyming Words
Comprehension Strategy: Story Structure
Think-Aloud Copying Master number 3

Before Reading

Genre: Tell children that you are going to read a well-known poem that is called a nursery rhyme, a short, rhyming poem for children. It is a Mother Goose nursery rhyme that children may be familiar with. Ask children if they know other nursery rhymes, such as "Humpty Dumpty" or "Jack and Jill."

Expand Vocabulary: The following words should be introduced before reading:

> *fleece:* the coat of wool on a sheep
>
> *lingered:* stayed
>
> *patiently:* without complaining

Set a Purpose for Reading: Have children listen for rhyming words in this nursery rhyme.

During Reading

Read through the poem the first time without interruptions. Then reread, drawing children's attention to the Think Aloud and the genre note.

Mary Had a Little Lamb

by Sarah Josepha Hale

Genre Study

Nursery Rhyme: Nursery rhymes not only have rhyming words, but they also have a certain rhythm that makes the poem pleasing to hear.

Mary had a little lamb,

Its <u>fleece</u> was white as snow;

And everywhere that Mary went,

The lamb was sure to go.

It followed her to school one day,

That was against the rule;

It made the children laugh and play

To see a lamb at school.[1]

And so the teacher turned it out,

But still it <u>lingered</u> near,

And waited <u>patiently</u> about

Till Mary did appear.

"Why does the lamb love Mary so?"

The eager children cry.

"Why, Mary loves the lamb, you know,"

The teacher did reply.

Think Aloud

[1]*I was able to picture in my mind the children laughing when they saw the lamb follow Mary to school. I think that the children at our school would act the same way.*

After Reading

Retell: Have children draw a picture to show what happens in the poem. Encourage them to use rhyming words to describe their pictures.

Student Think Aloud

Use Copying Master number 3 to prompt children to tell what they were able to visualize as they listened to this poem.

> "I was able to picture in my mind . . ."

Cultural Perspective

A sheep is usually sheared or shaved once a year. The wool fleece is cleaned and spun into yarn. Products such as sweaters, coats, and blankets are made from wool. The wool industry is important to many countries around the world, including Australia, Argentina, and the United States.

Think and Respond

1. What do you think the rule is about animals at Mary's school? *Possible response: There are no pets allowed at school.* **Inferential**

2. There are many pairs of rhyming words in this nursery rhyme. Name some. *Possible reponses: snow, go; day, play; rule, school; out, about; near, appear; so, know; cry, reply* **Genre**

3. What do you think the author wants you to know about Mary and her lamb? *Possible response: They love each other and hate to be apart from each other.* **Author's Purpose**

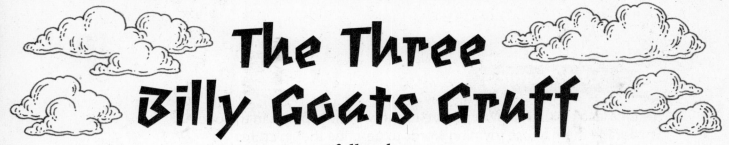

The Three Billy Goats Gruff

a folk tale

retold by Carolyn Quattrocki

Genre: Folk Tale

Comprehension Strategy: Story Structure

Think-Aloud Copying Master number 3

 Before Reading

Genre: Tell children that "The Three Billy Goats Gruff" is a folk tale. A folk tale is a story that people have told over and over again. This story was first told in the country of Norway. Explain that "The Three Billy Goats Gruff" has been told so many times that no one is really sure who the author is.

Expand Vocabulary: To help children understand this folk tale, introduce these words before reading:

> *braid:* three strands of material woven together
>
> *troll:* in fairy tales, a creature that lives in a cave or underground
>
> *evil:* mean, bad
>
> *meadows:* grassy lands

Set a Purpose for Reading: Have children listen to the story to find out how the goats cross a bridge.

 During Reading

Use the Think Alouds during the first reading of the story. Notes about the genre and cultural perspective may be used during subsequent readings.

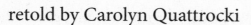

The Three Billy Goats Gruff

retold by Carolyn Quattrocki

Once there were three Billy Goats Gruff. The oldest was Big Billy Goat Gruff who wore a collar of thick black braid. Middle Billy Goat Gruff had a red collar around his neck, and Little Billy Goat Gruff wore a yellow one.

Big Billy Goat Gruff had a deep, gruff billy goat voice. Middle Billy Goat Gruff had a middle-sized billy goat voice. And Little Billy Goat Gruff had a very high, little billy goat voice.

All winter long, the three Billy Goats Gruff lived on a rocky hillside. Right next to their hill ran a powerful, rushing river.[1]

Every day during the cold winter months, the three Billy Goats Gruff played among the rocks.

Little Billy Goat Gruff would cry in his little billy goat voice, "Watch this!" as he leaped over the rocks.

Middle Billy Goat Gruff would call, "Watch this!" as he leaped over the middle-sized rocks.

Big Billy Goat Gruff would say in his big billy goat voice, "WATCH THIS!" as he leaped over great big rocks.

At night the wind would blow over the three Billy Goats Gruff. Little Billy Goat Gruff looked up to see a sky filled with bright, shining stars.

Middle Billy Goat Gruff looked up at the night to see the thin sliver of a winter moon.

Big Billy Goat Gruff said, "Enough looking at the sky. It is time to find a place to sleep."

So the three Billy Goats Gruff found a nice, cozy cave to sleep in. They lay down together on the cold winter nights and dreamed of springtime.

Soon it was springtime. From their rocky hillside the three Billy Goats Gruff looked longingly across the rushing river.

"How I would love to go up the mountain across the river," said Little Billy Goat Gruff. "The grass is green, and the flowers are pretty. There is plenty to eat on that side."

"To get to the mountain," said Middle Billy Goat Gruff, "we will have to cross the bridge over the river."

Think Aloud

[1] When I am rushing, I am moving very fast. Knowing this helps me understand what a rushing river is. It is water that is moving very quickly. A rushing river would be hard to swim across.

Genre Study

Folk Tale: The characters in folk tales often include animals acting and speaking like people, just like the three goats in this story.

Think Aloud

[2] I was able to picture in my mind what the troll looks like because the author gives a good description of the troll's eyes, hair, and nose.

Think Aloud

[3] I wonder what plan Big Billy Goat Gruff has to get across the bridge. I wonder how the billy goats will trick the troll.

The three Billy Goats Gruff knew that under the bridge lived a great, ugly <u>troll</u>. The troll had eyes that were as big as saucers, a head of shaggy hair, and a nose that was long as a broomstick.[2] Every day the Billy Goats Gruff looked across the river.

"The grass looks so sweet over there!" said Little Billy Goat Gruff. "Let's go over the bridge."

"The flowers smell like honey!" said Middle Billy Goat Gruff. "Yes, let's go over the bridge."

"But what are we to do about the troll?" asked Big Billy Goat Gruff. They all shook their heads sadly.

One day, as they were looking at the green mountain, Big Billy Goat Gruff had an idea. He thought of a plan to trick the troll so that they could cross the bridge to the other side.[3]

The next morning the three Billy Goats Gruff went down to the river. Little Billy Goat Gruff started to cross the bridge.

Trip-trap, trip-trap, trip-trap went Little Billy Goat Gruff's feet on the bridge.

"Who's that trip-trapping across my bridge?" roared the troll.

"It is only I, Little Billy Goat Gruff," said Little Billy Goat Gruff.

"I'm coming to eat you up!" said the troll.

"Oh no!" said Little Billy Goat Gruff. "I am only a tiny, little billy goat. Wait for my brother, Middle Billy Goat Gruff. He will make a much bigger dinner for you."

So the troll let Little Billy Goat Gruff cross the bridge to the other side.

In a little while Middle Billy Goat Gruff started across the bridge. Trip-trap, trip-trap, trip-trap went Middle Billy Goat Gruff's feet as he walked across the bridge.

"Who's that trip-trapping across my bridge?" roared the troll.

"It is only I, Middle Billy Goat Gruff," he said.

"I'm coming to eat you up!" said the troll.

"Oh no!" said Middle Billy Goat Gruff. "I am only a middle-sized billy goat. Wait for my brother, Big Billy Goat Gruff. He will make a much bigger dinner for you to eat."

The troll let Middle Billy Goat Gruff cross the bridge to the other side.

Finally Big Billy Goat Gruff crossed the bridge. TRIP-TRAP, TRIP-TRAP, TRIP-TRAP went Big Billy Goat Gruff as he walked on the bridge.

"Who's TRIP-TRAPPING across my bridge?" roared the troll.

"It is I, Big Billy Goat Gruff," he said.

"I'm coming to eat you up!" said the troll.

"Come ahead!" said Big Billy Goat Gruff. So the troll climbed up onto the bridge. Then Big Billy Goat Gruff, with his two big horns, tossed the troll high into the air, and he fell down into the river below.

The three Billy Goats Gruff were happy to be on the other side. They feasted on the green grass and wildflowers.

"I was right," said Little Billy Goat Gruff. "The grass tastes as sweet as it smells."

"And I was right, too," said Middle Billy Goat Gruff. "The flowers are like honey."

"Best of all, I was right," said Big Billy Goat Gruff. "We tricked the evil troll and used the bridge."

So the three Billy Goats Gruff spent their summer happily eating in the high meadows. They grew very fat and contented.

When the weather began to grow cold again in the autumn, the three fat Billy Goats Gruff came down from the high meadows.

This time they crossed over the bridge without a worry. After Big Billy Goat Gruff tossed him into the river, the wicked troll was never seen again.

Retell the Story: Have children act out the story. Assign the roles of the three Billy Goats Gruff and the troll.

Student Think Aloud

Use Copying Master number 3 to prompt children to share pictures they remember from a scene in the folk tale.

"I was able to picture in my mind . . ."

Cultural Perspective

Statues of trolls are popular souvenirs for tourists who visit Norway. One kind of troll, called a *Nisse,* is thought to bring good luck to the family who shows kindness to it.

Think and Respond

1. Which Billy Goat do you think was the bravest one? Why? *Responses will vary.* **Analytical**

2. Folk tales often have parts that repeat themselves. What activity is repeated in this folk tale? *Possible response: A goat crosses a bridge and meets a troll three times.* **Genre**

3. What do you think the author wants to teach you with this story? *Possible response: Don't be afraid to use your imagination to solve a problem.* **Author's Purpose**

UP, UP, UP! IT'S APPLE-PICKING TIME

a story

by Jody Fickes Shapiro

Genre: Fiction

Comprehension Strategy: Story Structure

Think-Aloud Copying Master number 6

Before Reading

Genre: Remind children that a story tells about a series of events, called the plot. It has characters and a setting. Some stories, like this one about a family who goes apple picking, could be true.

Expand Vocabulary: The following words will help children understand the story's setting:

> *orchard:* land with fruit trees on it
>
> *aroma:* smell
>
> *cider:* a drink made from apple juice
>
> *brim:* the rim of a container

Set a Purpose for Reading: Have children listen to the story to find out what a child does during apple-picking time.

During Reading

Use the Think Alouds during the first reading of the story. Notes about the genre and cultural perspective may be used during subsequent readings.

UP, UP, UP! IT'S APPLE-PICKING TIME

by Jody Fickes Shapiro

"Up, up, up! It's apple-picking time." Mama's voice tickles my ear, whispers me awake.

On with my shirt, sweater, pants, warm socks, and shoes not tied.

Outside it feels as if we're the only ones awake in the whole world. Dad says, "It's a long drive ahead."

Amber uses my shoulder for her pillow. But I don't mind. She's keeping me warm while we're driving, driving, driving to the apple ranch.

Two picnics later—one for breakfast, one for lunch—we're finally off the highway and onto the twisting, bumpy, narrow bridge (one car only) apple-tree-lined road.

There they are! Granny and Grandpa, standing at the gate, calling, "Hooray! We're so glad you're finally here. We could hardly wait."

"Neither could we," we say.

Then everyone is off to the <u>orchard</u>.

It's apple-picking time.

Apple smell is in the air—apple perfume everywhere.

There are so many trees and it looks like a million apples—red, green, yellow, and pink. "I don't know where to start," I tell Grandpa.

He pulls a yellow apple off a tree, puts it up to his nose, and breathes in like Mama does with a flower. "Ah, it's perfect apple <u>aroma</u>," says Grandpa, and we lean in close and smell it, too.

From his pocket he takes out his red-handled knife and cuts a slice out of the apple.

"Have a taste," he says.

The apple is cool and crunchy and sweet. Everyone has a slice, and we all stand together in the afternoon sunshine, wishing we could have more.[1]

But it's apple-picking time.

Think Aloud

[1] I thought the descriptions were important in this story because they help me use my senses to help me pretend I am in the orchard. I can smell the perfume of the apples. I can see many different colors of apples! I can even taste them!

"Begin with this Golden Delicious, Myles," Grandpa tells me. He points to the tree where we're standing and hands me a small sack made from cloth.

I give the littlest tug and the yellow fruit almost falls into my hand. It's as big as my softball.

The sack gets heavy fast. Every time it's full, I empty it into a wooden field box.

We climb up ladders and disappear into the trees. I can see Dad's legs. His voice is coming from the middle of a tree filled with red apples. He's singing a made-up song about loving apple dumplings and eating apple pie.

The tree next to him has Mama's laugh. That's the only way I can tell she's in it.

Amber and Granny are picking up fruit from the ground. Granny says these apples make the best cider.

The mention of cider makes me want some. It's warm work, picking apples. I say that it already smells as if cider is hiding somewhere in the orchard.

"That's apple-orchard perfume you're smelling, Myles," says Granny. Then she surprises us with cups of cool apple juice.

All afternoon we fill those apple sacks with Delicious—both red and golden—McIntosh, Pippin, Winter Banana (a funny name for an apple, if you ask me), and the last few stray Gravensteins.

The wagon cart is loaded with boxes filled to the brim.

Daylight runs out fast in that canyon, even in summer.

Granny's Pippin pie makes a fine end to an apple-picking day. Early to bed. Have to be well rested for an apple-selling day.

"Up, up, up! It's apple-selling time." Grandpa's whiskers scratch my cheek, and the smell of breakfast cooking pulls me out of bed.

It's Grandpa's morning oatmeal with sweet applesauce. Then we're out to the fruit stand through the dew-wet grass.

Grandpa turns over the carved wooden sign. Cars pull in.

Granny, wearing a big straw hat trimmed all around with shiny apples, greets old friends. "These are the grandkids come to help." She almost sings the words.

Apples are tasted, admired, and bought.

We carry bags and boxes of apples to cars for the people who come and go all morning. Lunch is a picnic in the sunshine, but we can hardly sit still enough to eat.

It's apple-selling time.

And then before you can say "McIntosh-Granny Smith-Golden Delicious-Pippin pie," the sun has flown away, taking the warmth with it. The sign is turned to "Closed." It's time to call it a day.

Supper is fresh-baked apple dumplings, floating like islands in a sea of milk. Then there's talking about that apple-selling day.

Grandpa puts old jazz records on his phonograph and dances around with Amber. Even Mama and Dad dance, but I like lying on the rug in front of the fireplace, just watching everyone being happy, wishing we didn't have to go home tomorrow.

It's hard to say good-bye—hello hugs are so much nicer.[2]

Sackfuls of apples surround Amber and me. We're driving, driving, driving home. Their cidery smell helps me remember the happy days of apple-picking—apple-selling time.

Think Aloud

[2] I can understand why the author says hello hugs are nicer than saying good-bye. My grandparents lived far away, too, and I hated it when we had to say good-bye.

After Reading

Retell the Story: Have children draw a picture to show their favorite part of the story. Have them describe their pictures.

Student Think Aloud

Use the Copying Master number 6 to prompt children to tell something that they thought was important in the story and why.

"I thought _____ was important in this story because . . ."

Cultural Perspective

There are more than seven thousand different varieties of apples grown around the world. China is the world's largest producer of apples.

Think and Respond

1. What do you think is the best job to have during apple-picking time? Why? *Responses will vary.* **Analytical**

2. Why does this story seem like it could happen in real life? *Possible responses: The characters in the story are like family members I know; it seems like something my family might do.* **Genre**

3. Why do you think the author wrote this story? *Possible response: to tell readers what happens when apples are ready to be picked from trees in the fall* **Author's Purpose**

Goldilocks and the Three Bears

a folk tale

retold by Jane Jerrard

Genre: Folk Tale

Comprehension Strategy: Summarize

Think-Aloud Copying Master number 7

Before Reading

Genre: Tell children that *Goldilocks and the Three Bears* is a folk tale. Remind them that a folk tale is a story that has been told over and over again.

Expand Vocabulary: Introduce the following words before reading:

> *porridge:* a hot cereal similar to oatmeal

> *wee:* tiny

> *wink:* a very short time

Set a Purpose for Reading: Invite children to listen to find out what happens when Goldilocks meets the three bears.

During Reading

Use the Think Alouds during the first reading of the story. Notes about the genre and cultural perspective may be used during subsequent readings.

Goldilocks and the Three Bears

retold by Jane Jerrard

There once was a family of three bears. There was a great big Papa Bear, a middle-size Mama Bear, and a wee little Baby Bear. The three bears lived in a cozy little house right in the middle of the forest.

The three bears always started each day in the very same way. First they washed their faces and paws with sparkling fresh water and sweet-smelling soap. Then they made their beds and fluffed their feather pillows. After they were dressed for the day, they went downstairs for a nice breakfast of delicious <u>porridge</u>.

One bright morning Mama Bear cooked the porridge and called her family for breakfast, just as she did every day, rain or shine. She spooned the porridge into their three bowls, and they all sat down to eat.

"It's too hot!" exclaimed Baby Bear, tasting the porridge in his <u>wee</u> little bowl.

"We must let the porridge cool for a little while," agreed Papa Bear and Mama Bear, after they tasted the porridge in their bowls.

The three bears decided to go for a walk while their hot breakfast cooled. Mama Bear took her basket in case they happened to find ripe blackberries to put on top of their porridge.

Now it just so happened that a little girl named Goldilocks was out walking in the woods that morning, all by herself.

She had been walking since quite early and was feeling rather tired. She was hungry as well, because she had left her house without eating breakfast. When Goldilocks saw the bears' little house, she thought it was the perfect place to rest.

Goldilocks marched up to the front door and knocked, but there was no answer. The bears were still out taking their walk. So Goldilocks just let herself in![1]

Goldilocks saw the three bowls of porridge. Her mouth started to water and her stomach started to rumble at once. She decided that she simply must taste the porridge.

First she dipped the spoon into the great big bowl that belonged to Papa Bear. "Ooo, this porridge is too hot!" she cried.

Think Aloud

[1] *So far this story is mostly about a family of bears who decide to go for a walk in the woods while their hot porridge cools. A girl named Goldilocks decides to take a rest and lets herself into the bears' home while they are away.*

Next she tried the middle-size bowl that belonged to Mama Bear. "This porridge is too cold!" she said.

Last she had a taste from the wee little bowl that belonged to Baby Bear. "This porridge is just right!" she said, and she gobbled it all up.

After she had eaten the porridge, Goldilocks wanted to rest. She went into the bears' sitting room, where she saw three chairs.

First she sat down in the great big chair. "This chair is too hard!" she said.

Next she tried the middle-size chair. "This chair is too soft!" she said, struggling to get out.

Last she tried the wee little chair that was just the right size for her to sit in. "This chair is just right!" she smiled. But Goldilocks sat down so hard that the wee little chair broke all to pieces!

By this time Goldilocks was very sleepy. She tiptoed up the stairs and found three beds.

First she lay down on the great big bed. "This bed is too high at the head!" she said.

Next she tried the middle-size bed. "This bed is too high at the foot!" she frowned.

Last Goldilocks lay down on Baby Bear's wee little bed. And she said, "This bed is just right!" Soon Goldilocks fell fast asleep.

A short time later the three bears returned home from their walk. They noticed right away that things were not quite right.

Papa Bear looked at his great big bowl of porridge and said in his great big voice, "Someone has been eating my porridge!"[2]

Think Aloud

[2] *The bear family has just come home to discover that someone had been in their house. I think they must be very angry.*

Mama Bear looked at her middle-size bowl of porridge and said in her middle-size voice, "Someone has been eating my porridge!"

Baby Bear looked at his wee little bowl and said in his wee little voice, "Someone has been eating my porridge AND HAS EATEN IT ALL UP!"

The three bears then went into their sitting room. When he saw his great big chair, Papa Bear said in his great big voice, "Someone has been sitting in my chair!"

Mama Bear looked at her middle-size chair and said in her middle-size voice, "Someone has been sitting in my chair!"

Baby Bear looked at his wee little chair and cried in his wee little voice, "Someone has been sitting in my chair AND HAS BROKEN IT ALL TO PIECES!"

The three bears went up the stairs to their bedroom. Papa Bear looked at his great big bed and said in his great big voice, "Someone has been sleeping in my bed!"

When Mama Bear looked at her middle-size bed, she said in her middle-size voice, "Someone has been sleeping in my bed!"

Baby Bear looked at his wee little bed and cried in his wee little voice, "Someone has been sleeping in my bed, AND THERE SHE IS!"

Baby Bear's wee little voice woke Goldilocks. She sat up to find three bears staring at her. They did not look pleased to see her!

Quick as a <u>wink</u>, she rolled out of bed and ran straight to the window.[3] She jumped right out and ran off as fast as her legs would carry her.

The three bears never saw Goldilocks again.

Think Aloud

[3] I like the phrase "quick as a wink." It takes a very short time to wink. That tells me how quickly Goldilocks reacted to seeing the bears.

After Reading

Retell the Story: Invite one child to be the narrator and retell the important events of the story. Have other children play Goldilocks and the three bears and act out the story.

Student Think Aloud

Use Copying Master number 7 to prompt children to summarize the story.

"This story was mostly about . . ."

Cultural Perspective

An earlier version of this folk tale comes from England and is entitled Scrapefoot. Scrapefoot is a fox who is curious about a family of bears who lives in the same woods as he does.

Think and Respond

1. How do you think Goldilocks felt when she woke up and saw the bears? *Possible responses: scared; embarrassed; confused* **Inferential**

2. What parts of this folk tale tell you that it is make-believe? *Possible response: The bears talk and act like people.* **Genre**

3. Why do you think the author wrote this story? *Possible response: to entertain readers* **Author's Purpose**

Make Way for Ducklings

a story

by Robert McCloskey

Genre: Fiction

Comprehension Strategy: Summarize

Think-Aloud Copying Master number 7

Before Reading

Genre: Remind children that a story that is made up is called *fiction*. Explain that *Make Way for Ducklings* takes place in a real city called Boston, in Massachusetts, but the author made up the characters and the events.

Expand Vocabulary: Introduce the following words before reading this story:

> *mallard:* a type of duck
>
> *island:* a piece of land surrounded by water
>
> *bank:* land that is at the edge of a pond, river, or lake
>
> *dither:* confused

Set a Purpose for Reading: Invite children to listen to find out who needs to make way for the ducklings.

During Reading

Use the Think Alouds during the first reading of the story. Notes about the genre and cultural perspective may be used during subsequent readings.

Make Way for Ducklings

by Robert McCloskey

Mr. and Mrs. Mallard were looking for a place to live. But every time Mr. Mallard saw what looked like a nice place, Mrs. Mallard said it was no good. There were sure to be foxes in the woods or turtles in the water, and she was not going to raise a family where there might be foxes or turtles. So they flew on and on.

When they got to Boston, they felt too tired to fly any further. There was a nice pond in the Public Garden, with a little island on it. "The very place to spend the night," quacked Mr. Mallard. So down they flapped.

Next morning they fished for their breakfast in the mud at the bottom of the pond. But they didn't find much.

Just as they were getting ready to start on their way, a strange enormous bird came by. It was pushing a boat full of people, and there was a man sitting on its back. "Good morning," quacked Mr. Mallard, being polite. The big bird was too proud to answer. But the people on the boat threw peanuts into the water, so the Mallards followed them all round the pond and got another breakfast, better than the first.

"I like this place," said Mrs. Mallard as they climbed out on the bank and waddled along. "Why don't we build a nest and raise our ducklings right in this pond? There are no foxes and no turtles, and the people feed us peanuts. What could be better?"

"Good," said Mr. Mallard, delighted that at last Mrs. Mallard had found a place that suited her. But—

"Look out!" squawked Mrs. Mallard, all a dither. "You'll get run over!" And when she got her breath she added: "This is no place for babies, with all those horrid things rushing about. We'll have to look somewhere else."

So they flew over Beacon Hill and the State House, but there was no place there.

They looked in Louisburg Square, but there was no water to swim in.[1]

Then they flew over the Charles River. "This is better," quacked Mr. Mallard. "That island looks like a nice quiet place, and it's only a little way from the Public Garden."

Think Aloud

[1] *This story was mostly about two ducks who are looking for a place to raise a family. They are looking for a safe place near a pond. Mrs. Mallard is not satisfied with the places she has seen. I wonder if the Mallards will find a safe place to raise their ducklings.*

"Yes," said Mrs. Mallard, remembering the peanuts. "That looks like just the right place to hatch ducklings."

So they chose a cozy spot among the bushes near the water and settled down to build their nest. And only just in time, for now they were beginning to molt. All their old wing feathers started to drop out, and they would not be able to fly again until the new ones grew in.

But of course they could swim, and one day they swam over to the park on the river bank, and there they met a policeman called Michael. Michael fed them peanuts, and after that the Mallards called on Michael every day.

After Mrs. Mallard had laid eight eggs in the nest she couldn't go to visit Michael anymore, because she had to sit on the eggs to keep them warm. She moved off the nest only to get a drink of water, or to have her lunch, or to count the eggs and make sure they were all there.

One day the ducklings hatched out. First came Jack, then Kack, and then Lack, then Mack and Nack and Ouack and Pack and Quack. Mr. and Mrs. Mallard were bursting with pride. It was a great responsibility taking care of so many ducklings, and it kept them very busy.

One day Mr. Mallard decided he'd like to take a trip to see what the rest of the river was like, further on. So off he set. "I'll meet you in a week, in the Public Garden," he quacked over his shoulder. "Take good care of the ducklings."

"Don't you worry," said Mrs. Mallard. "I know all about bringing up children." And she did.

She taught them how to swim and dive.

She taught them to walk in a line, to come when they were called, and to keep a safe distance from bikes and scooters and other things with wheels.

When at last she felt perfectly satisfied with them, she said one morning: "Come along, children. Follow me."[2]

Before you could wink an eyelash Jack, Kack, Lack, Mack, Nack, Ouack, Pack and Quack fell into line, just as they had been taught. Mrs. Mallard led the way into the water and they swam behind her to the opposite bank.

There they waded ashore and waddled along till they came to the highway.

Mrs. Mallard stepped out to cross the road. "Honk, honk!" went the horns on the speeding cars. "Qua-a-ack!" went Mrs. Mallard as she tumbled back again. "Quack! Quack! Quack!

Think Aloud

[2] *Mrs. Mallard and the ducklings are going to meet Mr. Mallard in the Public Garden. I wonder what will happen on their adventure to the Public Garden.*

Quack!" went Jack, Kack, Lack, Mack, Nack, Ouack, Pack, and Quack, just as loud as their little quackers could quack. The cars kept speeding by and honking, and Mrs. Mallard and the ducklings kept right on quack-quack-quacking.

They made such a noise that Michael came running, waving his arms and blowing his whistle.

He planted himself in the center of the road, raised one hand to stop the traffic, and then beckoned with the other, the way policemen do, for Mrs. Mallard to cross over.

As soon as Mrs. Mallard and the ducklings were safe on the other side and on their way down Mount Vernon Street, Michael rushed back to his police booth.

He called Clancy at headquarters and said: "There's a family of ducks walkin' down the street!" Clancy said: "Family of *what*?" "*Ducks*!" yelled Michael. "Send a police car, quick!"

Meanwhile Mrs. Mallard had reached the Corner Book Shop and turned into Charles Street, with Jack, Kack, Lack, Mack, Nack, Ouack, Pack, and Quack all marching in line behind her.

Everyone stared. An old lady from Beacon Hill said: "Isn't it amazing!" and the man who swept the streets said: "Well, now, ain't that nice!" and when Mrs. Mallard heard them she was so proud she tipped her nose in the air and walked along with an extra swing in her waddle.

When they came to the corner of Beacon Street there was the police car with four policemen that Clancy had sent from headquarters. The policemen held back the traffic so Mrs. Mallard and the ducklings could march across the street, right on into the Public Garden.[3]

Inside the gate they all turned round to say thank you to the policemen. The policemen smiled and waved good-bye.

When they reached the pond and swam across to the little island, there was Mr. Mallard waiting for them, just as he had promised.

The ducklings liked the new island so much that they decided to live there. All day long they follow the swan boats and eat peanuts.

And when night falls they swim to their little island and go to sleep.

Think Aloud

[3] *At first I thought that maybe the police officers would capture the ducklings. But then here I find out that they want to help the ducklings cross the street. I think the policemen are very nice to the ducks.*

After Reading

Retell the Story: Use questions like these to help children retell the story: *What happens first? What happens next? Where does the Mallard family go next?*

Student Think Aloud

Use Copying Master number 7 to prompt children to summarize the story.

"This was mostly about . . ."

Cultural Perspective

People around the world describe the sound a duck makes in many different ways. In China, ducks say "gua gua"; in France, ducks say "coin coin"; and in Italy, ducks say "qua qua."

Think and Respond

1. How do you think the people of Boston feel about Mrs. Mallard and her ducklings? *Possible response: The people of Boston want to protect Mrs. Mallard and her ducklings from getting hurt.* **Inferential**

2. How can you tell that this story is not real? *Possible response: The ducks are married and they talk.* **Genre**

3. Why do you think the author wrote this story? *Possible response: He probably likes ducks and wanted to tell an interesting story about them.* **Author's Purpose**

The Little Red Hen

retold by Margaret H. Lippert

Genre: Folk Tale

Comprehension Strategy: Summarize

Think-Aloud Copying Master number 7

 Before Reading

Genre: Remind children that a folk tale is a story that has been told over and over again. Tell children that they will be reading another more contemporary version of the folk tale later in the day. Have them compare the two versions.

Expand Vocabulary: Introduce the following words before reading the folk tale:

> *ground:* crushed, broken into a powder
>
> *mill:* a flour-making factory where wheat is ground into flour

Set a Purpose for Reading: Have children listen to find out what happens when the little red hen asks for help.

 **During Reading**

Use the Think Alouds during the first reading of the story. Notes about the genre and cultural perspective may be used during subsequent readings.

The Little Red Hen

Retold by Margaret H. Lippert

ONCE UPON A TIME a dog, a cat, a mouse, and a little red hen all lived together in a cozy little house. One day the little red hen found some grains of wheat in the yard.

"Who will plant this wheat?" asked the little red hen.

"Not I," said the dog.

"Not I," said the cat.

"Not I," said the mouse.

"Then I will do it myself," said the little red hen.

And she did. The wheat grew taller and taller. It turned from green to gold. At last it was time to cut the wheat.

"Who will cut this wheat?" asked the little red hen.

"Not I," said the dog.

"Not I," said the cat.

"Not I," said the mouse.

"Then I will do it myself," said the little red hen.

And she did. After the wheat was cut, it was ready to be ground into flour.

"Who will take this wheat to the mill?" asked the little red hen.[1]

"Not I," said the dog.

"Not I," said the cat.

"Not I," said the mouse.

"Then I will do it myself," said the little red hen.
And she did.

The little red hen carried the flour back to her house.

"Who will make this flour into bread?" asked the little red hen.

"Not I," said the dog.

"Not I," said the cat.

"Not I," said the mouse.

"Then I will do it myself," said the little red hen.[2]

Think Aloud

[1]I don't think the hen will get any help from the other animals. They did not help her plant or cut the wheat.

Think Aloud

[2]This was mostly about a little red hen who grew some wheat and had it made into flour without getting any help from the other animals.

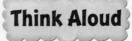

And she did.

When the bread was finished, the little red hen took it out of the oven. The cozy little house was filled with a delicious smell.

The dog and the cat and the mouse came running to the kitchen.

"Who will eat this bread?" asked the little red hen.

"I will!" said the dog.[3]

"I will!" said the cat.

"I will!" said the mouse.

"Oh no, you will not!" said the little red hen.

"You did not help me plant the wheat. You did not help me cut the wheat. You did not help me take the wheat to the mill. You did not help me bake the bread. And now you are not going to help me eat it. I am going to eat it all by myself."

And she did.

Think Aloud

[3] *I notice that the pattern in this story has changed. Instead of saying, "Not I," the dog says, "I will!" I wonder if the hen will let the dog eat the bread.*

After Reading

Retell the Story: Invite children to retell the story by acting it out. Assign the roles of the hen, dog, cat, and mouse.

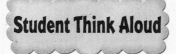

Use Copying Master number 7 to prompt children to summarize the story.

"This story was mostly about . . ."

Cultural Perspective

Bread comes from all around the world and in many shapes and sizes. In France, people eat flaky, crescent-shaped rolls called *croissants*. In Mexico, people eat flat, round corn tortillas. In England, people often eat triangle-shaped biscuits called *scones*. Americans enjoy all of these breads too.

Think and Respond

1. Do you think the little red hen was right not to share the bread? *Responses will vary. Possible responses: Yes, because the other animals did not help her make it. No, because we should always share with others.* **Critical**

2. How are the animals in this folk tale like the animals in other stories you have heard? *Possible response: They talk and act just as people do.* **Genre**

3. What lesson does the author want you to learn from this folk tale? *Possible responses: Always help others. If you do not help others, then they won't want to share with you.* **Author's Purpose**

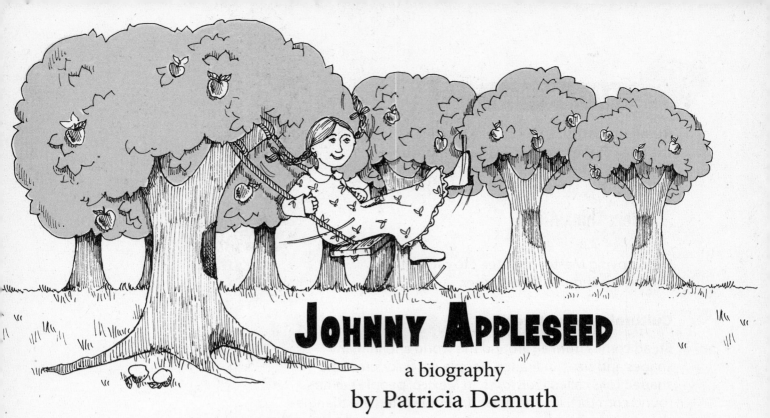

JOHNNY APPLESEED

a biography
by Patricia Demuth

Genre: Biography

Comprehension Strategy: Summarize

Think-Aloud Copying Master number 7

 Before Reading

Genre: Tell children that they will listen to a biography. A biography is a true story about a real person's life, but it is written by another person. Johnny Appleseed is the nickname of a special man named John Chapman.

Expand Vocabulary: Introduce the following words before reading:

  bloomed: produced flowers

  ripe: ready to be picked or eaten

Set a Purpose for Reading: Have children listen to find out why Johnny Appleseed is famous.

 During Reading

Use the Think Alouds during the first reading of the story. Notes about the genre and cultural perspective may be used during subsequent readings.

Johnny Appleseed

by Patricia Demuth

Who was Johnny Appleseed? Was he just in stories? No. Johnny was a real person. His name was John Chapman. He planted apple trees—lots and lots of them. So people called him Johnny Appleseed.

Johnny was young when our country was young. Back then many people were moving West. There were no towns, no schools, not even many houses. And there were no apple trees. None at all.

Johnny was going West, too. He wanted to plant apple trees. He wanted to make the West a nicer place to live. So Johnny got a big, big bag. He filled it with apple seeds. Then he set out.

Johnny walked for days and weeks. On and on. Soon his clothes were rags. His feet were bare. And what kind of hat did he wear? A cooking pot! That way he didn't have to carry it.

Snow came. Did Johnny stop? No. He made snowshoes. Then he walked some more.

Spring came. Johnny was out West now. He stopped by a river. He dug a hole. Inside he put an apple seed. Then he covered it with dirt. Someday an apple tree would stand here. Johnny set out again. He had lots more seeds to plant.[1]

Johnny walked by himself. But he was not alone. The animals were his friends.

Most people were afraid of wild animals. They had guns to shoot them. But not Johnny. One day a big, black bear saw Johnny go by. It did not hurt Johnny. Maybe the bear knew Johnny was a friend.

The Indians were Johnny's friends, too. They showed him how to find good food—berries and plants and roots.

Where did Johnny sleep?[2] Under the stars. Johnny liked to lie on his back and look up. The

Think Aloud

[1]*This story was mostly about how Johnny Appleseed went West all by himself and planted appleseeds so people would have a nice place to live.*

Think Aloud

[2]*The author asks me questions throughout the biography. It helps me know what I will be hearing about in the next few sentences. The questions give me a purpose for listening.*

wind blew softly. Owls hooted. The stars winked down at him.

Many years passed. Johnny planted apple trees everywhere. People started to call him Johnny Appleseed. One day he came back to where he had planted the first seed. It was a big tree now. A girl was swinging in it.³

That night Johnny stayed with the girl's family. He told stories. Everybody liked Johnny. "Stay with us," they said. "Make a home here." But Johnny did not stay. "I have work to do," he said. "I am happy. The whole world is my home."

More and more people came out West. Johnny planted more and more trees. In the spring, the trees bloomed with white flowers. In the fall, there were apples—red, round, ripe apples.

People made apple pies. And apple butter for their bread. And apple cider to drink. And children had apple trees to climb.

It was all thanks to Johnny Appleseed.

After Reading

Retell: Have children write a fact that they learned about Johnny Appleseed. Then have children read their facts to the class.

Student Think Aloud

Use Copying Master number 7 to prompt children to summarize their favorite part of the biography.

"This story was mostly about . . ."

Cultural Perspective

People all over the world eat apples. The apple is the world's most popular fruit. Early settlers brought apple trees and seeds to America from Europe. Apples were grown in New England just ten years after the Pilgrims arrived from England.

Think and Respond

1. What words would you use to describe Johnny Appleseed? *Possible responses: kind; thoughtful; friendly; hard-working* **Analyze**

2. How do you know this selection is a biography? *Possible response: It tells true facts about a real person.* **Genre**

3. Why do you think Patricia Demuth wrote this story? *Possible response: She wanted people to know more about Johnny Appleseed.* **Author's Purpose**

We're Going on a BEAR HUNT

a story

by Michael Rosen

Genre: Fiction (Poem)

Comprehension Strategy: Summarize

Think-Aloud Copying Master number 4

Before Reading

Genre: Remind children that a *fiction* story tells about make-believe events. The story they will hear looks and sounds like a poem and is about searching for a bear. Also, the readers are characters.

Expand Vocabulary: Introduce the following words before reading:

oozy: squishy

stumble: to fall or trip

narrow: not wide

Set a Purpose for Reading: Ask children to pretend that they really are on a bear hunt. Also have them listen for the language patterns and chime in when they can.

During Reading

Use the Think Alouds during the first reading of the story. Notes about the genre and cultural perspective may be used during subsequent readings.

We're Going on a
BEAR HUNT

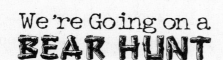

by Michael Rosen

We're going on a bear hunt.
We're going to catch a big one.
What a beautiful day!
We're not scared.

Oh-oh! Grass!
Long, wavy grass.
We can't go over it.
We can't go under it.

Oh, no!
We've got to go through it!

Swishy swashy!
Swishy swashy!
Swishy swashy!

We're going on a bear hunt.
We're going to catch a big one.
What a beautiful day!
We're not scared.

Oh-oh! A river!
A deep, cold river.
We can't go over it.
We can't go under it.

Oh, no!
We've got to go through it!

Splash splosh!
Splash splosh!
Splash splosh![1]

Think Aloud

[1] The author uses words that match the sounds we would hear if we were really going through grass or a river. These sound words are fun to say.

We're going on a bear hunt.
We're going to catch a big one.

What a beautiful day!
We're not scared.

Oh-oh! Mud!
Thick, oozy mud.
We can't go over it.
We can't go under it.

Oh, no!
We've got to go through it!

Squelch squerch!
Squelch squerch!
Squelch squerch!

We're going on a bear hunt.
We're going to catch a big one.
What a beautiful day!
We're not scared.

Oh-oh! A forest!
A big, dark forest.
We can't go over it.
We can't go under it.

Oh, no!
We've got to go through it!

Stumble trip!
Stumble trip!
Stumble trip!

Genre Study

Fiction: This story has four lines that are repeated over and over again like the chorus of a song.

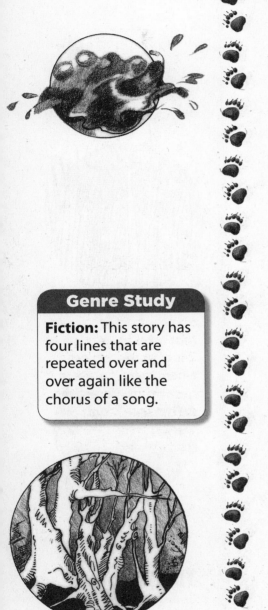

We're going on a bear hunt.
We're going to catch a big one.
What a beautiful day!
We're not scared.

Oh-oh! A snowstorm!
A swirling, whirling snowstorm.
We can't go over it.
We can't go under it.

Oh, no!
We've got to go through it!

Hoooo woooo!
Hoooo woooo!
Hoooo woooo![2]

We're going on a bear hunt.
We're going to catch a big one.
What a beautiful day!
We're not scared.

Oh-oh! A cave!
A narrow, gloomy cave.
We can't go over it.
We can't go under it.

Think Aloud

[2] *This story was mostly about a hunt for a bear that takes us through lots of outdoor places where there is grass, a river, mud, a forest and even a snowstorm. I wonder what we'll go through next.*

Oh, no!
We've got to go through it!

Tiptoe!
Tiptoe!
Tiptoe!
WHAT'S THAT?

One shiny wet nose!
Two big furry ears!
Two big goggly eyes!
IT'S A BEAR!!!!

Quick! Back through the cave! Tiptoe!
    Tiptoe! Tiptoe!

Back through the snowstorm! Hoooo
    woooo! Hoooo woooo!

Back through the forest! Stumble trip!
    Stumble trip! Stumble trip!

Back through the mud! Squelch
    squerch! Squelch squerch!

Back through the river! Splash splosh!
    Splash splosh! Splash splosh!

Back through the grass! Swishy
    swashy! Swishy swashy![3]

Get to our front door.
Open the door.
Up the stairs.

Oh, no!

We forgot to shut the door.
Back downstairs.

Shut the door.
Back upstairs.
Into the bedroom.

Into bed.
Under the covers.

We're not going on a bear hunt again.

Think Aloud

[3] *I figured out that the writer is taking us back the same way we came because he uses the word "back" and the order of places we visited is reversed. He also shows how fast we are traveling because of the scary bear!*

After Reading

Retell the Story: Invite children to retell the story by acting out the hunters on their search for the bear through grass, river, and other elements.

Student Think Aloud

Use Copying Master number 4 to prompt children to share something that they figured out from listening to the story.

"I figured out _____ because . . ."

Cultural Perspective

Tell children that they can go on bear hunts on four continents: North America, South America, Europe, and Asia. They can look for eight different species or kinds of bears.

Think and Respond

1. How do you feel each time you hear the words "We're not scared"? *Responses will vary.* **Analyze**

2. How is this story different from other stories you have listened to? *Possible response: It seems like the reader is actually part of this story.* **Genre**

3. Why do you think Michael Rosen wrote this story? *Possible response: He wanted to entertain readers.* **Author's Purpose**

HABITATS: Where Animals Live

from *World Almanac for Kids*

Genre: Nonfiction

Comprehension Strategy: Summarize

Think-Aloud Copying Master number 5

 **Before Reading**

Genre: Remind children that *nonfiction* books and articles give true facts about something. Explain that they will hear a nonfiction article about places where animals live.

Expand Vocabulary: To help children understand the descriptions of the animal habitats, explain the following words:

habitat: the place where an animal lives

regions: large areas of land

humid: damp or moist

climate: the weather conditions of a place over a long period of time

Set a Purpose for Reading: Tell children to listen to find out what habitat their favorite wild animal lives in.

 During Reading

Use the Think Alouds during the first reading of the selection. Notes about the genre and cultural perspective may be used during subsequent readings.

HABITATS: Where Animals Live

from *the World Almanac for Kids*

The area in nature where an animal lives is called its **habitat**. Some large habitats and some of the animals that live in them are:

Deserts (hot, dry regions): camels, bobcats, coyotes, kangaroos, mice, Gila monsters, scorpions, rattlesnakes

Tropical Forests (warm, humid climate): orangutans, gibbons, leopards, tamandua anteaters, tapirs, iguanas, parrots, tarantulas

Grasslands (flat, open lands): African elephants, kangaroos,[1] Indian rhinoceroses, giraffes, zebras, prairie dogs, ostriches, tigers

Mountains (highlands): yaks, snow leopards, vicunas, bighorn sheep, chinchillas, pikas, eagles, mountain goats

Polar Regions (cold climate): polar bears, musk oxen, caribou, ermines, arctic foxes, walruses, penguins, Siberian huskies

Oceans (sea water): whales, dolphins, seals, manatees, octopuses, stingrays, coral, starfish, lobsters, many kinds of fish

Genre Study

Many nonfiction books and articles list definitions that explain important words so that readers or listeners can better understand a topic.

Think Aloud

[1] *I noticed that the author used a short description of each habitat after the habitat's name. The description is simple and easy to understand.*

Retell: Have children list one or two facts they learned about habitats while listening to the selection.

Student Think Aloud

Use the Copying Master number 5 to prompt children to share something they noticed the author did.

"I noticed the author . . ."

Cultural Perspective

The wild Bactrian, or two-humped camel, is facing extinction in the Gobi Desert of Mongolia. People use these camels for transportation, food, shelter, and clothing.

Think and Respond

1. Which habitat would you like to live in? What animal would you like to be? Why? *Possible response: I would like to be a parrot in a tropical forest because they are colorful and can fly.* **Analyze**

2. How is this selection different from the biography about Johnny Appleseed? *Possible response: It is organized as a list and not about a person's life.* **Genre**

3. Why might the author have presented the information as a list? *Possible response: to make the information easier to understand* **Author's Purpose**

The Hokey Pokey

a song

by Roland Lawrence LaPrise

Genre: Song

Comprehension Strategy: Visualize

Think-Aloud Copying Master number 3

Before Reading

Genre: Tell children that the selection, "The Hokey Pokey," is actually a song and a dance. Invite children to tell when or where they might have heard the song before.

Expand Vocabulary: Introduce these words to children before you begin reading:

> *chorus:* a part of a song that is repeated over and over
>
> *backside:* the back of the body

Set a Purpose for Reading: Ask children to picture themselves dancing the "Hokey Pokey."

During Reading

Use the Think Alouds during the first reading of the song. Notes about the genre and cultural perspective may be used during subsequent readings.

The Hokey Pokey

Genre Study

Song: The chorus is a group of lines that are repeated after each verse. Because these lines are repeated several times, it saves room on the page to just write the word *chorus*.

You put your right hand in,

You put your right hand out,

You put your right hand in,

And you shake it all about.

You do the hokey pokey

And you turn yourself around.

That's what it's all about.

Hey!

You put your left hand in, etc.[1]
Chorus

You put your right foot in, etc.
Chorus

You put your left foot in, etc.
Chorus

You put your big head in, etc.[2]
Chorus

You put your backside in, etc.
Chorus

Think Aloud

[1] *I like this song because it helped me learn my right side from my left side when I was little.*

Think Aloud

[2] *I was able to visualize moving different parts of my body in and out of a circle.*

After Reading

Retell: Invite children to take turns saying (or singing) the verses of the song as other children perform the dance. If possible, play the song and have children sing and dance along.

Student Think Aloud

Use Copying Master number 3 to prompt children to share something they visualized while listening to the song.

"I was able to picture in my mind . . ."

Cultural Perspective

In England, Hokey-Pokey is a traditional name for ice cream. It was called this because the Italian vendors selling ice cream would call out, "Ecco un poco," which means "Here is a little" in Italian.

Think and Respond

1. Pretend you are the author of this song. What is another verse that you could add to the song? *Possible response: You put your right knee (or elbow) in.* **Critical**

2. How is this song like a poem? *Possible responses: Parts of it are repeated over and over again; it has rhyming words.* **Genre**

3. Why do you think the author wrote the song? *Possible response: It is a fun song that gets everyone up and moving around.* **Author's Purpose**

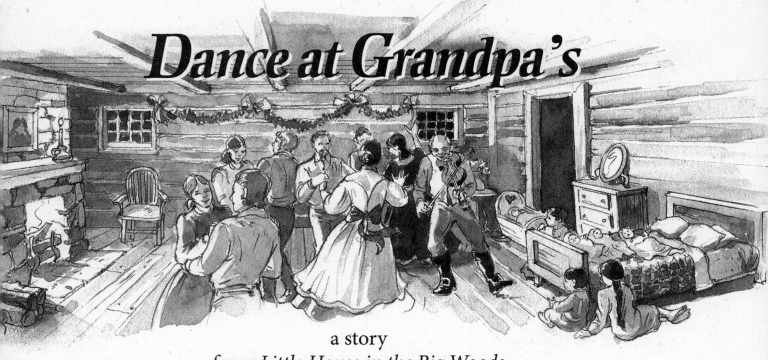

Dance at Grandpa's

a story

from *Little House in the Big Woods*

by Laura Ingalls Wilder

Genre: Historical Fiction

Comprehension Strategy: Visualize

Think-Aloud Copying Master number 3

Before Reading

Genre: Historical fiction is a story about something that happened in the past. The author uses her imagination to make up the characters and what they say, but some of the events in the story may have really happened.

Expand Vocabulary: Introduce the following words or terms before reading:

>*snug:* comfortable, cozy
>
>*feather bed:* a mattress stuffed with feathers
>
>*hickory:* a type of tree
>
>*on foot:* walking

Set a Purpose for Reading: Have children listen to find out how people had fun together long ago.

During Reading

Use the Think Alouds during the first reading of the story. The genre note may be used during subsequent readings.

Dance at Grandpa's

from *Little House in the Big Woods*
by Laura Ingalls Wilder

Once upon a time, a little girl named Laura lived in the Big Woods of Wisconsin in a little house made of logs. She lived there with her Pa, her Ma, her big sister Mary, her baby sister Carrie, and their good old bulldog Jack.

One winter morning everyone got up early, for there was going to be a big party at Grandpa's house. While Laura and Mary ate their breakfast, Pa packed his fiddle carefully in its box and put it in the big sled waiting by the gate.

The air was frosty cold, but Laura, Mary, Carrie, and Ma were tucked in <u>snug</u> and warm under robes in the sled. The horses pranced, the sleigh bells rang merrily, and they went off through the Big Woods to Grandpa's house.[1]

It did not seem long before they were sweeping into the clearing at Grandpa's house. Grandma stood at the door smiling and calling them to come in.

Laura loved Grandma's big house. It was fun to run from the fireplace at one end of the big room all the way to Grandma's soft <u>feather bed</u> on the other side.

The whole house smelled good. There were sweet and spicy smells coming from the kitchen, and the smell of <u>hickory</u> logs burning with bright, clear flames in the fireplace.

Before long it was time to get ready for the party. Laura watched while Ma and the aunts made themselves pretty. They combed their long hair and put on their best dresses. Laura thought Ma was the most beautiful of all in her green ruffled dress.

Soon people began to come to the party. They came <u>on foot</u> through the woods with their lanterns, and they came in sleds and wagons. Sleigh bells were jingling all the time.

The big room was filled with tall boots and swishing skirts, and there were ever so many babies lying in rows on Grandma's feather bed. Laura thought Baby Carrie was the prettiest.

Then Pa took out his fiddle and began to play. All the skirts began to swirl and the boots began to stamp. "Swing your partners!" Pa called.[2]

Think Aloud

[1] *There must be snow on the ground since the author says it is "frosty cold" and they are traveling in a sled. I wonder what it would be like to travel somewhere in a sled pulled by a horse. I think it would be fun!*

Think Aloud

[2] *I can picture in my mind the men in tall boots and the women in their swishing skirts. I can also picture the babies lying on the bed. Their parents must be dancing.*

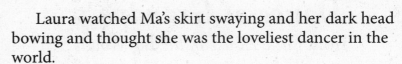

Laura watched Ma's skirt swaying and her dark head bowing and thought she was the loveliest dancer in the world.

Soon it was time for dinner. The long table was loaded with pumpkin pies, dried-berry pies, and cookies. There was cold boiled pork and salt-rising bread. How sour the pickles were! They all ate until they could eat no more.[3]

The fiddling and dancing went on and on until it was time for Laura and the other children to go to bed.

When Laura woke up, it was morning. There were pancakes and maple syrup for breakfast, and then Pa brought the horses and sled to the door.

Pa tucked Laura and Mary and Carrie and Ma into the sled. Grandma and Grandpa stood, calling, "Good-bye! Good-bye!" as they rode away into the Big Woods, going home. What a wonderful party it had been!

Think Aloud

[3] I notice the author tells how different foods look, taste, and smell. I think she does this so I can understand what it really felt like to be at the party.

After Reading

Retell the Story: Ask children to draw a picture of their favorite scene from the story. Then have them use their pictures to retell the story.

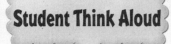

Use Copying Master number 3 to prompt children to share what they were able to visualize while they listened to the story.

"I was able to picture in my mind . . ."

Think and Respond

1. How is the party in this story the same or different from a party people might attend today? *Possible response: A party today might have different music and people might not wear ruffled dresses.* **Analyze**

2. What is the setting of this historical story? How does the author make it seem real? *Possible responses: The setting is a pioneer house in Wisconsin where Laura's grandparents live. The author makes it seem like a real place by telling how things look and smell, and even taste.* **Genre**

3. Why do you think someone would want to write stories about his or her own childhood? *Possible responses: to share memories, to show people what life was like during that time* **Author's Purpose**

One Monkey Too Many

a story

by Jackie French Koller

Genre: Rhyming Story

Poetic Element: Rhyme and Rhythm

Comprehension Strategy: Visualize

Think-Aloud Copying Master number 3

 Before Reading

Genre: Explain to children that this rhyming story is like a long poem. The rhyming words create a rhythm that makes the story fun to read.

Expand Vocabulary: Introduce the following words before reading the story:

> *pike:* a road
>
> *jammed:* pushed hard on the brakes
>
> *smugly:* acting too pleased with oneself
>
> *bellman:* a person who handles luggage at a hotel

Set a Purpose for Reading: Have children listen to find out what kinds of trouble monkeys can get into when there is "one monkey too many." In addition have them listen for the pattern and repetition and chime in when they can.

 **During Reading**

Use the Think Alouds during the first reading of the story. The genre note may be used during subsequent readings. Read the story in an expressive tone to emphasize the rhyme and rhythm of certain words.

One Monkey Too Many

by Jackie French Koller

"One," said the bikeman.
"This bike is for one.
One monkey can ride it,
and one can have fun."

But as soon as the bikeman
went back to his shop . . .

One monkey too many
jumped on the bike.
One monkey too many
wheeled off down the pike.

"Hooray!" the two shouted.
"We're having such fun.
This bike is far better for two
than for one!"

Then, bingo! The bike
hit a bump in the road . . .

It started to wobble.
It started to pitch.
One monkey too many
crashed into the ditch!

"Two," said the golfer.
"This cart is for two.
If you're looking for fun,
this is perfect for you."

But as soon as those rascals
climbed into their seats . . .

One monkey too many
hopped up in between.
One monkey too many
rolled off 'cross the green.

"Yippee!" They all wiggled
and giggled with glee.
"This car made for two
is fun-tastic for three!"[1]

Think Aloud

[1] *I was able to picture in my mind those three silly monkeys by the things they say and do when they climb into the golf cart.*

Genre Study

Rhyming Story: The author uses words in the title that have an easy rhythm and are fun to say. Then she repeats the title over and over again in the poem.

Think Aloud

[2]*I hear lots of rhyming words in this story, like* four *and* more. *The words make the story fun to listen to.*

They zoomed up a hill
and they started back down.
Then . . .

"Oh no!" they exclaimed,
as they jammed on the brake!
One monkey too many
splashed into the lake.

"Three," said the boatman.
"This canoe is for three.
There's a seat on each end
plus one more, don't you see?"

But just as the boatman
was pushing them off . . .

One monkey too many
swung into the boat,
one monkey too many
aboard and afloat.

They paddled quite nicely
away from the shore.
"See," they said smugly,
"it's just fine with four."

But soon up ahead
came the roar of the falls . . .

"Yikes!" they all screeched,
and they tried hard to stop.
But one monkey too many
had quite a long drop.

"Four," said the waiter.
"This table's for four.
You'll be far too crowded
if you try to fit more."[2]

But, of course, while the waiter
was getting their drinks . . .

One monkey too many
squeezed into a seat.
One monkey too many
demanded to eat.

"See here," they declared,
at the waiter's return,

"five fit just fine.
Please do not be concerned."

Then out came the dinners
and forks started flying . . .

Drinks spilled and plates tumbled,
and monkeys got rude.
One monkey too many
got covered with food.

"Five," said the bellman.
"This bed is for five.
I cannot allow
any more to arrive."[3]

But the minute the bellman
unloaded their bags . . .

One monkey too many
poked out his small head.
One monkey too many
crept into the bed.

"See," they agreed,
with a stretch and a yawn,
"we all fit quite nicely.
The bellman was wrong."

But as soon as they started
to toss and to turn . . .
. . . to kick and to twist
and to sputter and snore,
one monkey too many
ended up in a war.

"Six," said the author.
"This book is for six.
The pages are full,
so no more of your tricks."

But that noon when the author
went out for some lunch . . .

One monkey too many came sneaking
and . . .
. . . LOOK!

One monkey too many
got into this book.[4]

Think Aloud

[3] Uh oh! I think I know what is going to happen next because of what has happened before. I think another monkey is going to show up and try to squeeze into the bed.

Think Aloud

[4] I notice that the author makes herself a charater in this story. That is a funny way to end it.

After Reading

Retell the Story: Have children draw a picture of their favorite part of the story. Have them use the pictures to retell the story event.

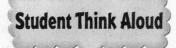

Use Copying Master number 3 to prompt children to share something they visualized during the story.

"I was able to picture in my mind . . ."

Think and Respond

1. How would you describe the monkey characters in this story? Why? *Possible response: They are very naughty because they cause trouble wherever they go.* **Critical**

2. How is the story similar to a poem? *Possible response: story rhymes and has a certain rhythm.* **Poetic Element**

3. Why do you think the author includes herself in the story? *Possible responses: It makes the story seem as if it is real; she wants to show that the monkeys don't listen to anybody!* **Author's Purpose**

Aiken Drum

a traditional song

Genre: Song
Poetic Element: Repetition and Rhythm
Comprehension Strategy: Visualize
Think-Aloud Copying Master number 3

Before Reading

Genre: Tell children that songs are words set to music. Explain to children that the song "Aiken Drum" has been sung for more than one hundred years. The song has a repeating chorus that creates a rhythm.

Expand Vocabulary: Introduce these terms before reading the song lyrics:

> *ladle:* a large spoon
>
> *penny loaves:* small loaves of bread
>
> *waistcoat:* a vest

Set a Purpose for Reading: Have children listen to find out what kinds of food Aiken Drum's clothing is made out of.

During Reading

Use the Think Alouds during the first reading of the story. Notes about the genre and cultural perspective may be used during subsequent readings. Emphasize the steady rhythm of the song by tapping a foot or swaying and nodding to the beat while reading.

Aiken Drum

There was a man lived in the moon, lived in the moon,
  lived in the moon,
There was a man lived in the moon,
And his name was Aiken Drum;
 And he played upon a <u>ladle</u>, a ladle, a ladle,
 And he played upon a ladle,
 And his name was Aiken Drum.

And his hat was made of good cream cheese, . . .
And his name was Aiken Drum;
 And he played . . .[1]

And his buttons were made of <u>penny loaves</u>, . . .
And his name was Aiken Drum;
 And he played . . .

And his coat was made of good roast beef, . . .
And his name was Aiken Drum;
 And he played . . .

And his <u>waistcoat</u> was made of crusts of pies, . . .[2]
And his name was Aiken Drum;
 And he played . . .

Genre Study

Rhythm: The chorus repeats at the end of each stanza. This repetition creates a rhythm that is easy to remember and follow.

Think Aloud

[1] *The repeating words make this song fun to hear. The sounds of the words make me feel like moving along to the music.*

Think Aloud

[2] *I was able to picture in my mind what Aiken Drum looked like by the way the author described his clothing. How silly he must look with all his clothes made out of food!*

Retell: Ask children to picture Aiken Drum in their minds as they retell what types of food make up his clothing. Then have them draw a picture of the character as they imagine him.

Student Think Aloud

Use Copying Master number 3 to prompt children to share what they think this song is mostly about.

"I was able to picture in my mind . . ."

Cultural Perspective

Tell children that this song was first published as an English nursery rhyme in 1841, more than 150 years ago. However, it may have been sung even earlier than that in Scotland. Help children recognize the cultural aspects of the piece.

Think and Respond

1. Aiken Drum wears clothing made out of food. What kind of food do you think his shoes might be made of? *Possible response: I think his shoes might be made of chocolate cake.* **Critical**

2. How is this song the same as other songs you know, such as "The Hokey Pokey"? *Possible response: It is a silly song that has repetition and rhythm.* **Genre**

3. Why do you think the author wants to teach you this song? *Possible responses: The author wants to introduce the readers to a song that has been around for a long time; the author wants people to have fun picturing a funny character.* **Author's Purpose**

Anansi Saves Antelope

an African fable
retold by Susan Kantor

Genre: Fable

Comprehension Strategy: Story Structure

Think-Aloud Copying Master number 1

Before Reading

Genre: Remind children that a fable is a story that teaches a lesson about life. Invite children to recall fables they have heard or read, such as "The Tortoise and the Hare."

Expand Vocabulary: Introduce these words before you begin reading:

savanna: flat open land without trees

panicked: became filled with fear

defenseless: helpless

thicket: a place where shrubs or small trees grow close together

Set a Purpose for Reading: Invite children to listen to find out the lesson the two characters learn about helping others. Have children listen for the tone of voice and content that signal friendly communication in your reading of the fable.

During Reading

Use the Think Alouds during the first reading of the story. Notes about the genre and cultural perspective may be used during later readings.

Anansi Saves Antelope

an African fable
retold by Susan Kantor

Doing a favor for a tiny creature eventually pays a big reward.

A bolt of lightning had started a fire. As it raged across the dry <u>savanna</u>, the animals <u>panicked</u>. Some were already surrounded by flames with no way to escape and others were running around frantically looking for a way to safety. While an antelope was looking for a way to escape she heard a tiny voice: "Please let me sit in your ear so you can carry me out of here."[1]

It was Anansi the Spider, and without waiting for an invitation, he jumped down from a branch and settled into the antelope's ear. There seemed to be fire everywhere, and the antelope had no idea of which way to go to avoid it. But the spider knew the way out, and he directed the antelope calmly and confidently: "Go to the left, now straight, now to the right . . ." until the antelope's swift legs had carried them both to safety across streams and brooks.

When the fire was far behind them, the spider ran down to the ground along the antelope's leg. "Thank you very much," he said. "I am sure we will meet again."

Sometime later, the antelope gave birth to a little baby. Like all baby antelopes, it was <u>defenseless</u> and spent most of its first few weeks hidden in the shrubs. Later, it could be seen grazing beside its mother. One day, two hunters spotted the mother antelope. While the little one crouched down under the shrubs, the mother leaped up to catch the hunters' attention, and then ran off, staying just out of range of their arrows.[2] After an hour the hunters gave up the chase, and went back to look for the baby antelope. Though they were sure they were searching in the right place, they eventually left the forest empty handed.

Much later, the mother came back. She, too, searched for the baby but could not find it. Then she heard a familiar voice calling her. It was the spider. Anansi led her to a <u>thicket</u> surrounded by a dense spider web. While the hunters had been chasing the mother, Anansi had been very busy weaving webs that had kept the baby invisible—and safe—from the hunters.[3]

Genre Study

Fable: In this fable, the lesson to be learned is clearly stated in the first sentence.

Think Aloud

[1] *I wonder who is talking to the antelope. It must be something very small because it has a tiny voice and can fit inside the Antelope's ear.*

Think Aloud

[2] *In the beginning the antelope helped Anansi escape the fire, then hunters came and chased the antelope. I wonder what will happen in the end.*

Think Aloud

[3] *Anansi wove a thick web around the area where the baby antelope was. The baby could not be seen. That must be what the word* invisible *means.*

After Reading

Retell the Story: Have partners work together and role-play Anansi and the antelope to retell the story. Invite volunteers to share their retelling with the class.

Student Think Aloud

"I wonder . . ."

Use Copying Master number 1 to prompt children to share a question they have about the fable.

Cultural Perspective

Anansi the Spider is a character often found in African fables. Anansi is known to play tricks to get what he wants.

Think and Respond

1. Why do you think Anansi helped the baby antelope? *Possible response: Anansi helped the baby because its mother helped Anansi.* **Inferential**

2. How is this fable like other fables you have read or heard? *Possible response: It has animal characters, and it teaches a lesson.* **Genre**

3. Why do you think the author wrote this story? *Possible responses: to teach us to always be ready and willing to help others; to show how helping others brings good things back to us.* **Author's Purpose**

Close Friends

a story

by Sally Lucas

Genre: Fantasy

Comprehension Strategy: Story Structure

Think-Aloud Copying Master number 6

Before Reading

Genre: Remind children that a fantasy story blends things that could be true with things that are make-believe. Animal characters often do things that humans can do. Remind children of another fantasy they have heard, "Beverly Billingsly Borrows a Book."

Expand Vocabulary: Introduce the following words before you begin reading the story:

>   *close:* near, familiar
>
>   *chirped:* made a short, shrill sound
>
>   *grin:* a smile

Set a Purpose for Reading: Have children listen to discover what two close friends do together. Guide children to recognize the tone of voice and content that signal friendly communication in your reading of the story.

During Reading

Use the Think Alouds during the first reading of the story. The genre note may be used during subsequent readings.

Think Aloud

[1]*I know that if I didn't feel good, a song and a present would cheer me up! I think the snowman will smile now.*

Think Aloud

[2]*In the beginning Squirrel and Bird couldn't make Snowman smile, then they called the children to help. I wonder what the children will do.*

Think Aloud

[3]*I thought the things the animals said were important in this story because they helped me understand how they felt and what they did. And hearing animals talk was fun. I could almost believe they were real!*

Close Friends

Squirrel and Bird were <u>close</u> friends. They went everywhere together. One day they saw a snowman standing alone in front of a house.

"Look at the sad snowman," said Squirrel. "Do you think we could cheer him up?"

"Of course," said Bird. "I'll sing to him. Music may make him feel better."

"I'll give him a present," said Squirrel. "That may cheer him up."[1]

Squirrel dug up some nuts he had been saving and laid them in a pile in front of the snowman. Bird sang her favorite songs. Still, the snowman didn't smile.

"We can't cheer him up," whispered Squirrel. "Maybe someone else can make him happy. Can you call the children in the house out to play? Maybe they will know what to do."[2]

Bird flew to the window and <u>chirped</u> as loudly as he could.

"Listen," cried a boy inside. "A bird is singing to tell us that it's a nice day. Let's go out and play."

Tom and his sister, Amelia, put on their jackets, boots, and mittens. They ran out to play in the snow.

They saw the nuts lying on the ground. "We can use these to give our snowman a bigger mouth," cried Tom. "He needs a smile on his face."

"And there will still be nuts left over," said Amelia. "Let's make another snowman. He can have a big <u>grin</u>, too."

Squirrel and Bird watched the children from a nearby tree.

"Look," said Squirrel to Bird. "You were right. The children knew what to do. The snowman is smiling."

"And they are making another snowman," chirped Bird.

"That's good," sighed Squirrel. "Everyone needs a close friend."[3]

After Reading

Retell the Story: Have children retell the story by acting it out. Assign roles of the squirrel, bird, snowman, and boy and girl.

Student Think Aloud

Use Copying Master number 6 to prompt children to share important details that helped them understand the fantasy.

"I thought _____ was important in this story because . . ."

Think and Respond

1. Why does the author say Squirrel and Bird were close friends? *Possible responses: They go many places together. They help each other and work together.* **Analyze**

2. How do you know this story is not real? *Possible responses: The animals talk. The animals try to help the snowman.* **Genre**

3. What does the author want you to know about friends? *Possible response: It is important to have a friend that you can talk to and do things with.* **Author's Purpose**

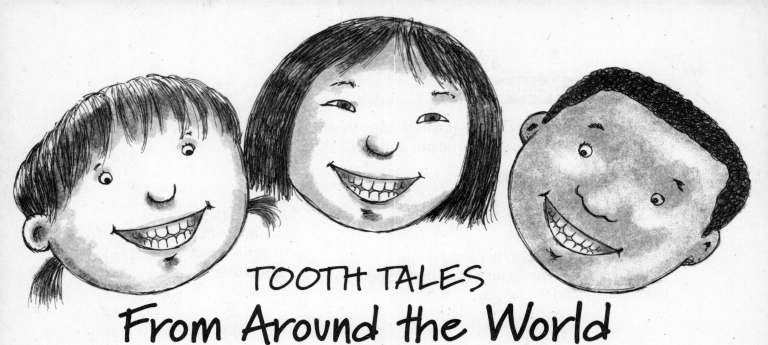

TOOTH TALES
From Around the World

by Margaret Tsubakiyama

Genre: Nonfiction

Comprehension Strategy: Text Structure

Think-Aloud Copying Master number 5

Before Reading

Genre: Explain to children that nonfiction selections tell true facts about people, places, and things. Nonfiction authors often use examples to help explain their topics. Remind children of the nonfiction story "Habitats: Where Animals Live," which they have heard.

Expand Vocabulary: Before reading, introduce these terms:

> *countries:* areas of land with boundaries and a shared government
>
> *bury:* to hide something in the ground
>
> *exchanges:* gives in return for something else

Set a Purpose for Reading: Invite children to listen to compare what they do when they lose a tooth to what other children around the world do.

During Reading

Use the Think Alouds during the first reading of the story. Notes about the genre and the cultural perspective may be used during subsequent readings.

Genre Study

Nonfiction: The writer uses examples from many countries to give the reader information about the meaning of losing a tooth.

TOOTH TALES
From Around the World
by Margaret Tsubakiyama

When you lose a tooth, you probably put it under your pillow and wait for the tooth fairy. Do you know what children in other <u>countries</u> do?

1. When a child in Japan loses a top tooth, he throws it on the ground. According to custom, this will cause the new tooth to grow in pointing down. If he loses a bottom tooth, he throws it on top of the roof. Now the new tooth will come in pointing up![1]

2. In Sri Lanka, children throw their teeth on the roof and ask the squirrels to take them away and bring them teeth as strong and sharp as the squirrel's teeth.

3. In Indonesia, children <u>bury</u> their teeth so their new teeth will "grow."

4. In Egypt, the water buffalo is an important animal known for its strong teeth. So when a child loses a tooth, he throws it into the sun and sings, "Take this ugly donkey's tooth you see, and bring a beautiful water buffalo's tooth for me!"[2]

5. In Germany, children save their teeth in a special "tooth box."

6. When a child in Holland loses a tooth, she invites her grandfather over. She stands with her back to him and throws him the tooth. Then the tooth "magically" turns into a coin and flies back to her!

7. In Africa, a child puts his tooth in a shoe, under his bed. While he sleeps, the "tooth mouse" comes and <u>exchanges</u> the tooth for money.[3]

8. In Denmark, children give their teeth to their parents. Their parents then set the teeth in gold or silver to make rings, necklaces, or pins.

Think Aloud

[1]*That tooth tale is really different from what I used to do when I lost a tooth. It sounds like a fun thing to do. I wonder what they do in other countries.*

Think Aloud

[2]*I noticed the author used lots of examples from different countries to make this article interesting. She even included a part of a song about teeth.*

Think Aloud

[3]*This sounds the most like what I did with my tooth as a child. I like the idea of a mouse coming to take the tooth. I wonder what a mouse would do with all the teeth.*

After Reading

Retell: Ask children to list a fact they learned about what children in other countries do when they lose a tooth.

Student Think Aloud

Use Copying Master number 5 to prompt children to share something they noticed about how the story was written.

"I noticed the author used . . ."

Cultural Perspective

Long ago in England and Australia, children would place their first baby tooth into a mouse hole. They believed that this would keep them from ever having a toothache.

Think and Respond

1. Which tooth tale did you find to be the most interesting? Why? *Responses will vary. Possible response: I liked the tale from Egypt because the rhyme made me laugh.* **Analyze**

2. What makes this selection nonfiction? *Possible responses: It is about something true; the author uses true facts and examples.* **Genre**

3. Why do you think the author wrote this story? *Possible response: She wrote it to share information about losing teeth.* **Author's Purpose**

THE TRIP BACK HOME

a story

by Janet S. Wong

Genre: Fiction

Comprehension Strategy: Story Structure

Think-Aloud Copying Master number 3

Before Reading

Genre: Remind children that a story tells about something that is fiction, or made up. Some stories, like this one, tell about things that could really happen.

Expand Vocabulary: Introduce these words before you read the story:

charcoal: a black material that is used as pencils for drawing and as fuel for heat

smoldering: burning and smoking without a flame

stalls: booths used for displaying and selling things

persimmons: orange-red fruits that grow on trees

Set a Purpose for Reading: As children listen to the story, ask them to think about what the author sees, hears, tastes, smells, and feels during her visit to Korea.

During Reading

Use the Think Alouds during the first reading of the story. Notes about the genre and the cultural perspective may be used during subsequent readings.

THE TRIP BACK HOME

by Janet S. Wong

The week we went on the trip back home
to visit the village where Mother grew up,
we shopped for gifts for our family,
things we thought they would need.

Then, in our brand-new traveling clothes,
we flew a day and a night and a day,
wiping our faces awake with hot towels
when we arrived in Korea.

We gave grandfather, my *haraboji*,
a pair of leather work gloves,
tough and tanned
like his thick-skinned farmer's hands.

We gave my grandmother, my *halmoni*,
an apron, ruffled at the edge,
with two large pockets
in the shape of flowers.

We gave my aunt, my *imo*,
a picture book with simple words
to teach her English.

They gave us hugs.[1]

Every morning
before the birds began to sing,
Haraboji woke me up
so I could watch him
push a fresh block of charcoal
into a tunnel near the house.
The charcoal sat smoldering on stones,
warming the air under the floor
while Mother slept late
those cold autumn mornings.

And always, every morning,
Haraboji let me wear his new leather gloves,
good for grabbing the charcoal
he made from stumps of trees.

Every day
before shopping with Halmoni,

I fed the hungry pigs
scraps of carrot and onion and egg
I rolled with rice.
I threw the sticky balls
as hard and as fast and as far as I could
so the running pigs would not
knock me down.[2]

Then Halmoni and I walked
up the rough dirt road to the outdoor market.
We searched through rows of tiny stalls
filled with clouds of rice cakes
and rivers of small soup fish
and hills of hot chili peppers,
searching for something crispy, fresh,
and cheap enough for five.

Back at the house
Halmoni made a fire in the stove
with pine branches I gathered.
Into a heavy iron pot
she measured the rice with a silver bowl
and I washed the rice
while she floated black sheets of seaweed
back and forth over an open flame
until the black turned to green.

Mother pulled spicy *kim chi* cabbage
from a cool clay jar
and set soup on the stove
to simmer.
Imo mixed mung bean sprouts
with sesame oil and sesame seeds
and garlic she had smashed
with a stone.[3]

After we ate
Halmoni and Mother and Imo and I
would sit in the afternoon sun,
sewing warm clothes for winter,
while Haraboji crouched on the roof,
sandwiching persimmons in straw,
where they would be stored all autumn.

And always, every day,
Halmoni let me wear her new ruffled apron,

Think Aloud

[2]*I was able to picture in my mind the pigs running at the author and trying to get at the food. I understand why she would throw the food and then run away from the pigs. I think I would be scared the pigs would knock me down, too!*

Think Aloud

[3]*This was mostly about all the different foods the family prepared. The author gives a lot of details, so I can almost taste and smell everything.*

good for holding spools of thread
and even better for hiding persimmons.

Every evening
before we unfolded our soft cotton beds,
we sat in a circle
on the smooth, warm *changpan*,
the oiled paper floor.

Sometimes we listened to Haraboji's stories,
with Mother laughing hard,
clutching her sides,
and me laughing hard, too,
to see her so happy.

Sometimes we played *hato*,
a game of cards
with pictures of flowers and deer
and hills and the moon.
Mother would slap the cards down,
shouting when she won.

And always, every evening,
Imo would find some quiet
and we would sit close,
reading her book together,
until we went to sleep.

This was how they passed the time
with us

and this was how we passed the time
with them

until the day came
to make our trip back home—

and Haraboji gave us
a charcoal drawing
of the hills behind the house,

and Halmoni gave us
dried persimmons strung together
in a necklace,

and Imo gave us
a poem in Korean,
folded small—

and we gave them hugs.

Genre Study

Korean Words: The author includes the Korean words that name her family, foods, and games that she played during her visit. This helps the reader know that the Korean people speak a different language than English.

After Reading

Retell the Story: Have children draw a picture to show something the author did on her visit to Korea. Have them tell about their drawings.

Student Think Aloud

Use Copying Master number 7 to prompt children to tell what a section of the story was mostly about.

"This story was mostly about . . ."

Cultural Perspective

Research with children some traditional Korean games and play them. Compare them to games that children are familiar with. Discuss with children how the author's background and cultural traditions influenced her writing. Help children recognize that the values, beliefs, and interests of an author are reflected in his or her literature. Encourage children to respect the ages, genders, and cultural traditions of the various authors they study.

Think and Respond

1. How are the events in this story the same as when you visit your grandparents or another relative? *Responses will vary. Possible responses: They also hug me when I visit them. I cook with them and help them with chores.* **Critical**

2. How is the story different from a fantasy? *Possible response: This story could really happen; a fantasy is about something make-believe.* **Genre**

3. Why do you think Janet Wong wrote this story? *Possible response: She wanted to share her experiences with her family in a different country.* **Author's Purpose**

Hide-and-Seek Shadow

a poem
by Margaret Hillert

Genre: Poem
Poetic Elements: Rhythm, Repetition
Comprehension Strategy: Visualize
Think-Aloud Copying Master number 3

Before Reading

Genre: Tell children that the words in a poem are often read with a certain rhythm or beat. The author repeats words to make the rhythm of the poem easier to hear. Remind children of other poems they have heard, such as "Growing Old" or "Just Watch."

Expand Vocabulary: Introduce these words before you begin reading the poem:

> *shadow:* dark shape cast on a wall or floor by something blocking light

> *cloud:* tiny water drops that form a large shape and float in the air above Earth

Set a Purpose for Reading: Have children listen for the rhythm of the poem, and imagine themselves moving in the ways the poet describes.

During Reading

Read through the poem the first time without interruptions. Notes about the Think Alouds, genre, and the cultural perspective may be used during subsequent readings.

Hide-and-Seek Shadow

by Margaret Hillert

I walked with my <u>shadow</u>,

I ran with my shadow,

I danced with my shadow,

I did.[1]

Then a <u>cloud</u> came over

And the sun went under

And my shadow stopped playing

And hid.

Genre Study

Rhythm: The author keeps the same rhythm in the first three lines and suddenly ends the fourth line. She repeats this same rhythm pattern in the next four lines of the poem.

Think Aloud

[1] *I am able to picture in my mind dancing outside and watching my shadow move the same way that I was moving. I have done this before, especially on a sunny day.*

After Reading

Retell: Have children act out the poem, moving to its rhythm as you reread it. Assign pairs to play the child and the shadow.

Student Think Aloud

Use Copying Master number 3 to prompt children to describe something that they can picture from listening to this poem.

"I was able to picture in my mind . . ."

Cultural Perspective

Long ago, people used shadows to tell time. The morning shadow would disappear around noon and then grow longer during the afternoon.

Think and Respond

1. What might cause the shadow to stop hiding and come back? *Possible response: When the sun comes back out the shadow will reappear.* **Inferential**

2. What words do you hear repeated over and over in the poem? *Possible response: with my shadow* **Genre**

3. Why do you think the author chose the title "Hide-and-Seek Shadow"? *Possible response: When the shadow appears and disappears, it seems as if you are playing a game of hide-and-seek with the shadow.* **Author's Purpose**

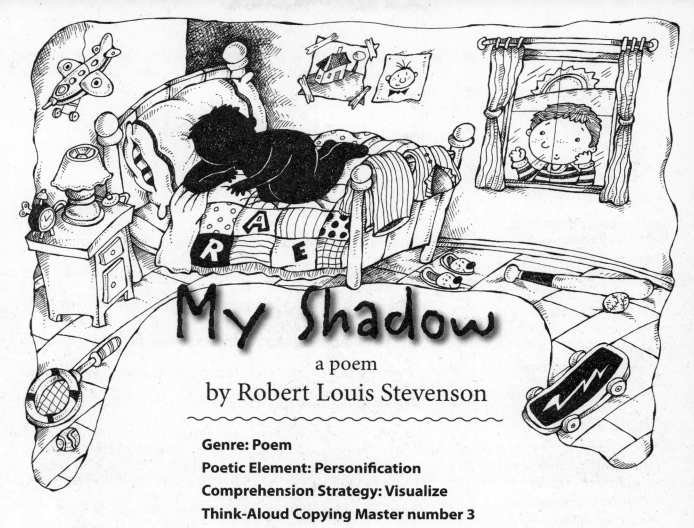

My Shadow

a poem

by Robert Louis Stevenson

Genre: Poem

Poetic Element: Personification

Comprehension Strategy: Visualize

Think-Aloud Copying Master number 3

 Before Reading

Genre: Point out that some poems describe something by making it seem human. This is called *personification*. Explain to children that they will hear a poem that describes a shadow this way.

Expand Vocabulary: Introduce the following words before reading this poem:

> *heels:* the back part of the feet
>
> *notion:* an idea
>
> *coward:* a person who is easily frightened
>
> *nursie:* a nanny; someone who takes care of a child
>
> *arrant:* behaving badly

Set a Purpose for Reading: Have children listen for examples of how the author personifies the shadow, or makes it seem human.

 **During Reading**

Read through the poem the first time without interruptions. Then reread, pausing to draw students' attention to the Think Alouds.

Genre Study

Personification: The author writes about the shadow as if it were a real boy. It makes the shadow seem alive.

Think Aloud

[1] *I was able to picture in my mind that the shadow is a little child because the author has it doing things a real child might. I can imagine him walking close behind the real child.*

Think Aloud

[2] *I figured out that the shadow isn't with him because the sun isn't up yet. You need the sun to be shining outside to have a shadow.*

My Shadow

by Robert Louis Stevenson

I have a little shadow that goes in and out with me,

And what can be the use of him is more than I can see.

He is very, very like me from the <u>heels</u> up to the head;

And I see him jump before me, when I jump into my bed.

The funniest thing about him is the way he likes to grow—

Not at all like proper children, which is always very slow;

For he sometimes shoots up taller like an India-rubber ball,

And he sometimes gets so little that there's none of him at all.

He hasn't got a <u>notion</u> of how children ought to play,

And can only make a fool of me in every sort of way.

He stays so close beside me, he's a <u>coward</u> you can see;

I'd think shame to stick to <u>nursie</u> as that shadow sticks to me![1]

One morning, very early, before the sun was up,

I rose and found the shining dew on every buttercup;

But my lazy little shadow, like an <u>arrant</u> sleepy-head,

Had stayed at home behind me and was fast asleep in bed.[2]

After Reading

Retell: Have children draw a picture of something the shadow did to make it seem like a person. Have them describe their pictures.

Student Think Aloud

Use Copying Master number 3 to prompt children to share something they visualized while listening to the poem.

"I was able to picture in my mind . . ."

Cultural Perspective

Robert Louis Stevenson grew up in Scotland. He was born in Edinburgh in 1850. Stevenson was a sickly child and spent much of his time with a nurse who loved to tell him stories and read books aloud.

Help children recognize the cultural and historical aspects of the poem. Point out to them where Scotland is on a map. Then have them discuss how Stevenson's background influenced his writing.

Think and Respond

1. What did you learn about the author's shadow? *Possible responses: It is just like the author. It grows and then gets smaller. It is a coward.* **Analytical**

2. What did the author personify, or make seem like a person? How did he do this? *Possible response: He made his shadow seem like a person by making it jump and follow the child around just as another child might.* **Text Structure**

3. What is the poet's purpose for writing this poem? *Possible response: He wanted to entertain readers by making them think about how their shadows can seem real.* **Author's Purpose**

All Kinds of Families
by Norma Simon

Genre: Nonfiction

Comprehension Strategy: Generate Questions

Think-Aloud Copying Master number 5

Before Reading

Genre: Tell children that nonfiction gives information about real people and events. Invite children to recall another nonfiction selection they have heard, "Tooth Tales from Around the World."

Expand Vocabulary: Introduce these terms before reading:

> *niece:* the daughter of your brother or sister
>
> *nephew:* the son of your brother or sister
>
> *relatives:* family members
>
> *relations:* family members

Set a Purpose for Reading: Invite children to listen for information that reminds each of them about his or her family.

During Reading

Use the Think Alouds during the first reading of the story. Notes about the genre and the cultural perspective may be used during subsequent readings.

All Kinds of Families

by Norma Simon

A family is YOU. And the people who live with you, and love you, and take care of you. There are all kinds of families, but your own is the one you know best.

Families come in all sizes, BIG FAMILIES, MIDDLE-SIZED FAMILIES, LITTLE FAMILIES.

Families come in all ages, too. Young families with young children. Middle-aged families with teen-aged children. Old families with grown-up children and grandchildren.

Families come with all kinds of people, different sizes, different ages. They make all kinds of families.

A family is people who belong together. Like husbands and wives and their children. Like mothers and children . . . like fathers and children. Like grandparents and grandchildren.

People who live together, love together, fight together and make up, work and play with each other, laugh and cry and live under one roof together . . . They are a family.

What's *special* about a family? It's the feeling you have about each other from living in the same place, sharing good times and bad times . . . growing together.

A family can be a mother, a father, and children who are growing up. A family can be a mother and her children, living, loving, working, and sharing. A family can be a father and his children, living, loving, working, and sharing.[1]

A big sister or a big brother taking care of other children . . . can be a family. And a father and a mother together, their children grown-up and away . . . can be a family.

Children who live far away send letters. They write, "I'll be home soon. Can hardly wait to see everybody."

They telephone, too. "Hi, Mom! Hi, Dad! How are you? I'll be home for the holidays."

Families like to come together, for holidays, birthdays, a wedding, for sad times, and for happy times.

When families get together, they talk a lot, they eat a lot, they laugh a lot.

When everyone has said good-bye, the home feels empty.

Family people have family names. Like mother, father, sister, brother, son, and daughter. Like cousin, aunt, uncle, <u>niece</u>, <u>nephew</u>, grandmother, and grandfather.

Genre Study

Nonfiction: Nonfiction selections contain many details about their subject. This author tells readers about all kinds of families so they understand that there is not just one meaning for the word *family*.

Think Aloud

[1]*I can see the author wants me to understand that it doesn't matter who makes up a family as long as they are living, loving, working, and sharing.*

Think Aloud

[2] I noticed the author used questions about my own family. I think she wants me to picture my family when I am reading this.

All your <u>relatives</u> and <u>relations</u> have these family names.

When families go visiting, you hear many family names. Names like Aunt Susan and Uncle Ed. Names for different grandparents, like Grandma Hall and Granny Baker.

Some children have many relatives and relations. Almost too many to remember. Some children have only a few, and it's easy to name every one.

Can you name your aunts? Uncles? Grandparents?

Do you know their first names?[2]

You are part of your family, of the caring . . . and the sharing and the loving.

From the time when you're a tiny baby, when you're growing up . . . all grown up. All your life, wherever you live, YOU are a part of a family.

A family is YOU and the people who live with you. That's one part of your family.

Some people in your family may live in different places. They are still your family.

Part of your family lives far away, in another city . . . in another part of town, or nearby . . . in a different house.

You visit them. They visit you. And you know that they are family people: Aunts, uncles, cousins, grandparents.

You are all part of one big family.

A mother or a father may live in a different place, a place not with their children. No matter how near or how far, you are still part of the same family.

Some families live in the same home for a long time. Other families move from place to place.

But in a family home, there are things people like to keep around them: family pictures, a special chair, books . . . pets . . . toys. They take these things from one home to another.

When you are grown up, you may begin your own family, a new family . . . a young family. When a mother and a father have a child or adopt a child, a new family begins.

And the *new* family becomes a part of all the old ones: Part of the mother's family. Part of the father's family.

People in old and new families like to tell each other where they are, what they are doing. They send letters, postcards, birthday cards.

A letter for you has YOUR last name on it. Lots of persons in a family share the same last name. But, maybe, not all of them. And some people who aren't even in the same family have the same last name. That happens!

Families last a long . . . long . . . time. New babies are born or are adopted. Some people die. There are husbands, new wives . . . comings together, and goings apart. There are changes, but families go on.

Families share special stories that family people like to tell and family people like to hear.

The stories make everyone part of the big family.

Are there stories told in your family? Maybe there are stories about you, something you did or said? Maybe you hear the same stories over and over. Some day . . . you'll tell them, too.[3]

Some uncles tell stories, funny stories, silly stories. Stories about mischief they did. Stories about adventures they had. Stories about people you know. And aunts tell you more stories, ones they know.

Families like to tell stories many times. The old stories are new to the youngest children. They listen and want to hear them again. Funny stories, sad stories, part of growing up in a family.

Sometimes members of a family don't see each other for a long time. Maybe it's because they live too far away. Or because families have fights and don't agree. Maybe people are working, and there is no time to be together.

But when a family *does* come together after a long time, they say things like: "Oh, how the children have grown!" "Your hair is still so curly . . ." "It's good to be together again." "I'd know your girl anywhere. I remember when you looked like that." And the family feeling is all around them like a strong, invisible circle.

When *you* need help, your family helps you. When your family needs help, *you* help them. People in a family help each other and try to take care of each other.

Yes, families are for caring . . . loving . . . sharing, far or near, big or little . . . all kinds of families.

All kinds of families—and yours is one of them. Your family is always part of you. You are always part of it.

A family is a special part of your life.

Think Aloud

[3]*I wonder if I really will tell stories to younger family members someday. When I am older, I'd like to share my stories.*

After Reading

Retell: Invite children to draw a picture of their family. As they share their picture, have them tell how their family is like the ones mentioned in the story.

Student Think Aloud

Use Copying Master number 5 to prompt children to share what they noticed about how the author explains families.

> "I noticed the author . . ."

Cultural Perspective

In China, many grandparents live in the same house with their grandchildren. Aunts and uncles may also live in the same house and share food and money.

Think and Respond

1. Why does the author say that families are a special part of your life? *Possible responses: Families love and care for you; family members share, work together, play together.* **Inferential**

2. How does the author present information about families? *Possible responses: She gives facts and examples; she asks questions.* **Genre**

3. What does Norma Simon want you to know about families? *Possible responses: Families come in all sizes. They keep in touch with each other. They help each other.* **Author's Purpose**

Aunt Minnie and the Twister

a story
by Mary Skillings Prigger

Genre: Realistic Fiction
Comprehension Strategy: Generate Questions
Think-Aloud Copying Master number 1

 ## Before Reading

Genre: Tell children that "Aunt Minnie and the Twister" is a realistic fiction story about events that could really happen. Explain that the author makes up the characters and their names, but everything that happens to them could happen in real life.

Expand Vocabulary: Introduce these words before reading the story:

root cellar: a room dug into the ground used to store vegetables

chores: jobs, tasks

twister: a tornado

johnny house: an outdoor bathroom

Set a Purpose for Reading: Ask children to listen to find out how the twister affects the lives of Aunt Minnie and the children who live with her. Encourage children to listen carefully so that they can tell how the story is different from a play or poem.

 ## During Reading

Use the Think Alouds during the first reading of the story. Notes about the genre and the cultural perspective may be used during subsequent readings.

Aunt Minnie and the Twister

by Mary Skillings Prigger

Minnie McGranahan lived in a little house on a little farm in Kansas.

She had nine orphaned nieces and nephews, and they all lived with her. They called her "Aunt Minnie."

As Aunt Minnie's kids grew, the little house became more and more crowded. Sometimes the kids were cross, and sometimes they complained. Minnie said, "Well, we don't have much room—but we have each other."[1]

When Minnie wanted her kids' attention, she stood on the front porch and rang an old school bell. CLANG, CLANG, CLANG went the bell. Aunt Minnie's kids came running.

The bell called them for supper. It said, "Don't be late."

It summoned them when there was trouble. "Come quick, the cows are out!" Aunt Minnie shouted.

The bell rang when there was company. "Wash up. Preacher Bill is here to call. Let's look like proper folks," Aunt Minnie said.

Come spring, Minnie and her kids planted and hoed the garden. They made a scarecrow and put Aunt Minnie's old dress and hat on it to frighten the birds away. "Can't have those birds harvesting our crops before we do," laughed Minnie.

In the summer, they picked corn, beans, tomatoes, and peas and canned them for the winter. "This will be good eating when it's cold outside," Aunt Minnie told her kids.

In the fall, when the leaves began to turn, Minnie and her kids picked apples. She showed the children how to make apple butter, applesauce, and apple cider.

They put turnips, potatoes, and carrots in barrels and stored them in the root cellar in the hill beside the house.

The younger kids resisted going into the root cellar. Little snakes and toads liked to hide in the cool places. The snakes slithered into cracks and corners. Toads jumped out when a hand reached inside the barrel.

But Aunt Minnie wasn't afraid. She would scoop up the critters in her apron and shake them outside.

When winter came and snow covered the ground, Minnie and the kids gathered the food they had stored in the root cellar. "Yum," they said when they spread apple butter on their bread. "It tastes just like summertime."

Think Aloud

[1] Wow! Nine children living in a little house would be very crowded! I can tell Aunt Minnie is a very loving person because she doesn't mind the crowded house.

Genre Study

Realistic Fiction: Some realistic stories take place in the past. This story takes place at a time in the past when root cellars were used to store vegetables because they were dark and cool. The vegetables would not spoil, or go bad.

One spring day, storm clouds rolled across the sky. Aunt Minnie told her kids, "We need to do our chores, but listen for the bell. If it looks like it's fixin' to storm bad, I'll ring the bell. You come running home."

The clouds got blacker and blacker. Lightning flashed. Minnie rushed to the front porch and rang the bell. CLANG, CLANG, CLANG. "Come quick!" it said. Minnie's kids came running from the hen house, from the barn, and from the garden.

Minnie pointed at the sky where a large funnel-shaped cloud was forming. "Twister!" she shouted. "Hold on to each other and run for the root cellar!"

The oldest kids grabbed the youngest. The ones in the middle grabbed each other. They all held on to Aunt Minnie as they pushed against the wind.

They tugged and pulled the cellar doors open, and fell in a heap on the root cellar floor. BANG! Aunt Minnie slammed the doors behind them.

SMACK! CRACK! went the hailstones against the doors. WHOOOSH roared the wind. The doors strained and groaned. Aunt Minnie and her kids huddled together in the dark. They were safe inside the root cellar.

No one said a word about snakes or toads.

Suddenly it was quiet. "Shhh," said Aunt Minnie. "Listen!" *Croak, croak. Croak, croak.* "It's the toads!" said one of the boys. "They're telling us the storm is over." "We made it!" the children cheered. "And we still have each other!" said Aunt Minnie. "Now, let's see what mischief the twister did."

They pushed open the cellar doors and spilled outside. They couldn't believe what they saw. "LAND SAKES!" exclaimed Aunt Minnie. "LAND SAKES!" exclaimed the kids.[2]

"I don't believe it," Aunt Minnie sighed. The twister had cut a path through the fields. Aunt Minnie's Model T Ford was on its side. The hen house and the scarecrow were gone. The chickens were scattered all over the farm. The cows were in the front yard.

Most amazing of all was Aunt Minnie's house. It was still standing. But it had been turned around! The front was facing the johnny house, and the back was in the front!

Aunt Minnie didn't say a word. She took the two littlest children by the hand and led her kids in a parade around the house.

First they walked one way. Then the other. They checked up and down and all around.

Think Aloud

[2]*I wonder what they saw. "LAND SAKES" sounds like a big surprise. I think it has something to do with the big twister.*

Finally Aunt Minnie announced, "Well, this will never do! We can't have a topsy-turvy house. We can't have the front door facing the johnny house.

"And we can't very well turn the house back around. So we will just have to make a new front. We can build another room onto the back. Our family is getting too big for this little house anyway." "Hurrah!" shouted the children.

So they sold two calves, a brood of chicks, and the next crop of corn to buy building supplies. Minnie hired a carpenter from town. He worked and worked, and Aunt Millie and all the kids pitched in. They all worked together to build the new room.

When the work was done, they had a picnic to celebrate the new room on the back of the old front of the little house. And Aunt Minnie's kids knew they had a home for as long as they wanted.[3]

And, most important, they had each other.

Think Aloud

[3]*This is mostly about how a strong family can stay strong even when a twister changes their home.*

 **After Reading**

Retell the Story: Separate children into three groups. Have children in the first group draw scenes from the beginning of the story; have the second group draw scenes from the middle; and have the third group draw ending scenes. Reread sections of the story as necessary. Have children hold up their pictures in the order that the events happened in the story. Starting with the first group, ask each child to say one sentence about their picture.

Student Think Aloud

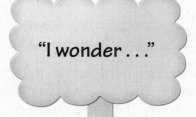

"I wonder . . ."

Use Copying Master number 1 to prompt children to share any questions they have about the story.

Cultural Perspective

While most tornadoes occur in the United States, they have been reported in Great Britain, India, Argentina, and other countries.

Think and Respond

1. Would you like to live with Aunt Minnie? Why or why not? *Responses will vary.* **Critical**

2. Even though the characters are from the author's imagination, why does this story seem real? *Possible response: A family could actually have to escape to a safe place like a root cellar to get away from a twister.* **Genre**

3. Why do you think the author wrote this story? *Possible responses: to show that family members can help each other through bad times; to show readers what life was like in the past.* **Author's Purpose**

Daddy Played Music for the Cows

a story
by Maryann Weidt

Genre: Realistic Fiction

Comprehension Strategy: Generate Questions

Think-Aloud Copying Master number 6

Before Reading

Genre: Explain to children that realistic fiction is a story that could happen in real life. The characters in the story are just like real people we might know. Invite children to recall other realistic fiction stories they have heard, such as "Aunt Minnie and the Twister."

Expand Vocabulary: Introduce the following words before reading the story:

rafters: sloping beams used to hold up a roof

crooned: sang softly

yodel: to sing so the voice changes back and forth from a low to a high note

silo: a tower used to store food for cattle

haymow: a hayloft

Set a Purpose for Reading: Encourage children to listen for the different types of music that Daddy liked to play for the animals in the barn.

During Reading

Use the Think Alouds during the first reading of the story. The genre note may be used during subsequent readings.

Daddy Played Music for the Cows

by Maryann Weidt

Mama always said I was born in the barn while Daddy played music for the cows. A bright red can full of seed corn was my rattle. It sang *kitch-ka-shoo, kitch-ka-shoo* when I shook it, while the cowboys sang on the radio and Daddy hummed along.

Mama set my playpen in the middle of the barn so I could listen to Daddy play music for the cows. When they strolled inside in slow motion, he picked me up and waltzed me down the aisle between them, patting their wide brown rumps and calling them by name—"Hey, Pearl Bailey, that's my girl . . . . Come on, Queenie . . . . Hello, Dolly"—as he nudged them into place.

The barn cats chased a sunbeam, and the kittens pushed their noses through my playpen bars. I shoved my nose out to meet them, and Daddy squirted warm milk at us while the radio sang "*yo-del-lay-hee-hoo*."[1]

One day the playpen went to the attic, but Daddy still played music for the cows. The chickens danced a two-step in the corner of the barn. I squatted down to see where the eggs came from, and as I watched, out one popped. I caught it with both hands. The shell was soft and brown and warm. When I gave it to Mama, she tucked it into her apron pocket while she sang "Golden Rings" along with the radio.

Sometimes when Daddy played music for the cows, trumpet sounds filled every crack in the barn. Sleeping pigeons looked up from under the eaves. The mourning doves sang *coo-ooh, coo, coo-coo* as they flew down from the <u>rafters</u>, picked bits of corn off the floor, and flew away. I chased after them, laughing, but never caught more than the feathers they dropped.

While Daddy scooped manure from behind each cow, Mama spread hay beneath them. "It's all right, Dolly," she <u>crooned</u>. Dolly nodded and swayed, her hot breath coming in time to the music, as someone on the radio sang about the moon.

When Daddy came in for dinner, he washed his hands and face and neck at the kitchen sink and combed his wavy black hair. "Horsie ride!" I said, and Daddy got down on all fours. I climbed onto his back and hung on to the straps of his overalls with both hands. "Giddyap, horsie!" I shouted. The cowboy on the radio sang, "*Happy trails to you*," and Daddy threw back his head and whinnied.

Think Aloud

[1]*The author includes made-up words that stand for the sounds that are heard in the barn. These words are fun to say and help me imagine what is happening in the story.*

Genre Study

Realistic Fiction: The characters in realistic fiction stories are involved in events that could really happen.

On my first day of first grade, I heard the cowgirls singing as I climbed off the bus and ran up the driveway. I changed my clothes as fast as I could, then raced for the barn. "Daddy!" I shouted. "I can read! Now I have to learn to yodel!"

All that year I listened to the cowgirls and tried to yodel just like them. I yodeled on the school bus. I yodeled when I fetched the cows from the pasture. I whirled and twirled and sang and yodeled and danced the chicken two-step down the center of the barn. "*Yo-del-lay-hee, yo-del-lay-heeee-hoooo*."[2]

In second grade, I worked on my daring circus act. While Mama and Daddy milked the cows, I climbed inside the silo and hung by my knees from the ladder till the smell of silage made me dizzy. Then, holding my nose with one hand, I waved my other to the crowd. Applause bounced up and down the tall, cool walls. A single sunbeam held me in its spotlight while Daddy turned the radio to "*Toe-ray-a-doe-ra!*"

Mama always told me, "Don't play in the haymow," but when Jackie Bonniwell dared me, I climbed to the top, grabbed the rope, and swung like Tarzan across the whole length of the barn. When I let go, I fell screaming into a feather bed of hay. I felt like I was tumbling along with the tumbling tumbleweeds.

For my eighth birthday party, my friends and I dressed up as cowgirls. In the barn, the radio played "*Git along, little dogies*" while we played hide-and-seek behind the cows. "It's okay, Queenie," I said. "It's my birthday."

When Mama called, "Cake and ice cream!" we joined arms, kicked our boots in the air, and danced across the yard, singing "*Whoopee ti-yi-yo.*"

When I was as tall as Daddy's armpit, I climbed onto the tractor and he showed me which levers to push and which to pull. Then I drove the tractor while Daddy and Mr. Bonniwell and Jackie put up hay. We worked all day and into the night to get the hay up before the rain. The music in my head sang one song after another: *Toe-ray-a-doe-ra...Happy trails to you...Yo-del-lay-hee-hoooooo.*

"Run and get the cows," said Daddy when the last load of hay was in the barn. I slid down the path to where Dolly and Pearl and Queenie were waiting with the others. I patted their soft warm bellies. Then, as they followed me to the barn, I lifted my chin and sang to the raindrops.

Daddy hugged me and laughed. "You look like a wet little muskrat," he said, "just like the day you were born." The air

Think Aloud

[2]*I wonder what the cows did when they heard all that yodeling. Since the father always played music for the cows, they probably liked the sound of the girl yodeling.*

smelled of wet cows and steaming manure. "Listen," said Daddy as he turned up the radio. A cowgirl was singing our favorite song. Daddy hummed along, his voice flat and happy, and I yodeled like I never had before, while Daddy played music for the cows.[3]

Think Aloud

[3]*I thought music was important in this story because the girl tells me all about the music she hears during different times in her life.*

After Reading

Retell the Story: Ask children to think about being an animal that lives in the barn and retell the story from how they see it. Ask the "animals" questions like "What do you hear?" or "What are the people doing?"

Student Think Aloud

Use Copying Master number 6 to prompt children to share something they thought was important in the story.

"I thought _____ was important because . . ."

Think and Respond

1. Why do you think Daddy liked to play music all the time? *Possible response: It made him and everyone else happy.* **Inferential**

2. How is this story different from a story like "Dance at Grandpa's"? *Possible responses: This story takes place in modern times. "Dance at Grandpa's" takes place long ago.* **Genre**

3. Why do you think the author chose the title "Daddy Played Music for the Cows"? *Possible response: It seems like a funny thing to do so you want to read the story to find out why he did it.* **Author's Purpose**

Bippity Bop Barbershop

a story
by Natasha Anastasia Tarpley

Genre: Realistic Fiction

Comprehension Strategy: Generate Questions

Think-Aloud Copying Master number 1

Before Reading

Genre: Remind children that realistic fiction is a story about something that could happen in real life. Explain to children that the author in the following story uses made-up characters to tell about a haircut experience. Discuss with children other examples of realistic fiction, such as "Daddy Played Music for the Cows."

Expand Vocabulary: Before reading, introduce these words:

"king me": a term used in checkers; a checker is placed on top of another one

ref: a referee, a person who enforces the rules in a game or sport

clippers: electric hair trimmers

dreadlocks: a hairstyle where hair is twisted into ropelike braids

Set a Purpose for Reading: Ask children to listen to this story to see if they have the same kinds of feelings as the main character, Miles, when they get a haircut.

During Reading

Use the Think Alouds during the first reading of the story. The genre note may be used during subsequent readings.

Bippity Bop Barbershop

by Natasha Anastasia Tarpley

Early Saturday morning, Daddy comes to wake me with our secret knock. *Bippity-be-bop-bop! Bippity-be-bop-bop!* "You up, Little Man?" Daddy pokes his head into my room. "I'm up!" I say excitedly and jump out of bed. I can hardly wait. I'm going to get my first haircut at the barbershop today!

Mama and my sister, Keyana, are still asleep. Daddy and I have the house all to ourselves.

Quietly, Daddy and I dress in matching blue jeans and gym shoes, then head outside.

We turn onto Main Street and stop at Jack's Sweet Shop. Daddy orders a gooey cinnamon roll and black coffee, and a glazed doughnut and chocolate milk for me. "Miles is getting his first haircut at the barbershop today," Daddy tells Mr. J. "Is that so?" Mr. J. asks, leaning over the counter. I nod yes. "This calls for a celebration. I'll make your milk a double." Mr. J pours chocolate milk into a tall cup. "Be brave, Little Man," he says as he hands it to me.

We eat as we walk. Up ahead I see the green and yellow awning and the white letters on the window that say SEYMOUR'S BARBERSHOP. Next to the door is a short, white barber's pole. It has red stripes, which curl and swirl around it like strange fish swimming in a sea of white.

And there's Mr. Seymour in the window, with his wild, gray hair, dusting off his big, shiny chair.

Mr. Seymour has been Daddy's barber since Daddy was a kid like me. Now, he'll be my barber, too.

Inside, the shop is crowded. Daddy stops to whisper something to Mr. Seymour, and then we walk to the back of the shop to find a seat. "Hey there, Charles!" "Hey there, Little Man!" "What's going on?" people call out as we pass. "First haircut?" one of the men asks me. I nod yes. "Nothing to it," he says. "Just gotta be brave."

All these people are telling me to be brave, but I don't know exactly what they mean. "What does 'brave' mean, Daddy?" I ask. "It just means that you're not afraid," Daddy says. When we sit down, I practice being brave.

As Daddy and I wait our turn, we watch two men playing checkers. *Slap!* One of the men slams his checker on the board. "King me!" he shouts with his arms raised high.

Another group of men is clustered around the television at the back of the shop watching a basketball game. "Come on, man, shoot the ball! What're you waiting for?" "Pass it, pass it!" "Foul! That was a foul! The ref must be blind!" "Whew, that boy can fly!" one man cheers when his favorite player finally makes a basket.

Jazz music, loud voices, and laughter blend with the *buzzzzzzzz* of clippers and the soft *sweesh-sweesh* whisper of scissors skimming loose hairs from a freshly cut head.[1]

I look at the men in the row of chairs in front of me. I can see their faces in the long mirror that runs along an entire wall of the shop. The man in Mr. Seymour's chair is getting his head shaved. "Take it all off," he says. A patch of sunlight gleams right on top of his bald head.

Another man has long, thick dreadlocks. He's getting a shave with a straight razor. When he leans all the way back in the chair, his locks almost touch the floor.

The next man is getting his hair cut low all around. The clippers go back and forth, dipping and gliding across his head, making smooth waves that ripple through his hair.

In the last chair, there's a kid, a little older than me, getting his big, curly Afro trimmed. "Just a little off the sides," he says.

But none of the styles I see look like me.

After a while, Mr. Seymour points toward Daddy and me and calls my name. *Me?!* I look at Daddy and then at Mr. Seymour and then at Daddy again. "You go first, Miles," he says and pats me on the shoulder. "Be brave, Little Man."

I can hear my heartbeat in my ears, and my knees feel wobbly. But I stand up and walk over to the chair.

Mr. Seymour helps me up, the chair is so high. Then he drapes a big, wide cape over me to catch the loose hairs. "What style would you like for your first haircut, Little Man?" Mr. Seymour asks. I shrug my shoulders. I don't know.

Mr. Seymour shows me a poster hanging on the wall with pictures of all kinds of different styles, but I still don't see any that look like me.

I take one more look around the shop, and when I see Daddy, I know right away which style I want: cut low on top and shaved clean all around, just like his. I whisper to Mr. Seymour, and he goes to work.

Think Aloud

[1]*This barbershop sure is a busy place! People are playing games, watching television, and getting haircuts! The author helps me picture in my mind people getting haircuts. She also helps me hear the sounds that Miles hears.*

Mr. Seymour takes out his pick. He picks my hair until it is fluffy and stands up high. Then, with his scissors, he begins to cut my hair just like Mama used to do at home.

But when he finishes with the pick and scissors, I hear him turn the clippers on. My heart starts beating fast again. *Will the clippers hurt? What if Mr. Seymour accidentally cuts off my ear?*

The loud buzzing noise is coming closer. Then I feel a tickle creeping up the back of my neck. I get so scared, I duck down as low as I can go in the chair and throw the cape over my head!

I peek out from under the cape when Mr. Seymour turns the clippers off. Daddy is squatting beside me. "I tried to be brave, but I didn't know how," I say with tears in my eyes.[2]

"You know, I was scared when I got my first haircut," Daddy says and wipes my tears away. "You were?" I say with my eyes open wide. Daddy nods.

"But I'll tell you a trick. Pretend that you're a giant, so tall your head touches the sky. And the buzzing of the clippers is just the sound of airplanes zooming by. Or maybe you're a superhero, saving the earth from a swarm of killer bees. Try it. I promise you won't be frightened anymore."

So I close my eyes and think about giants and my favorite superheroes. But I can't picture any of them getting a haircut. Then I remember watching Daddy get his hair cut, the way he sits up tall and closes his eyes halfway, like he doesn't have a care in the world. I think about how brave Daddy is, and I get brave, too.

When Mr. Seymour turns the clippers back on, I imagine that I have Daddy's long legs and wide shoulders. I sit up straight like Daddy, though I still squeeze the arms of the chair tightly.

And when Mr. Seymour is through, there is a brand-new me staring back from the mirror!

Mr. Seymour rubs a dab of a sweet-smelling blue aftershave on my face and the back of my neck. It feels like a cool breeze. Then he dips a brush in powder and gently sweeps it over my head and neck.

Daddy takes his seat in Mr. Seymour's chair. And when Mr. Seymour asks him how he wants his hair, Daddy says that he wants a haircut just like mine. Daddy wants to look like ME!

When Mr. Seymour is finished, Daddy and I smile at each other in the mirror. "You're sure we're not twins?" Daddy asks, raising one eyebrow.

Think Aloud

[2]*I wonder what the father will say to Miles. So far he's been taking good care of Miles and helping him feel happy, so I don't think he will be angry with Miles for hiding.*

On the way out, some of the other men in the shop hold their hands up to me for high fives. "Looking sharp, man," they say. "Guess I can't call you Little Man anymore, Miles. You're one of the big boys, now," Mr. Seymour says and shakes my hand. "See you next time."

I hum a happy, proud song as we leave Mr. Seymour's shop. *Bippity bop. Bippity-be-bop-bop.*[3] Daddy picks up the tune. We walk to the rhythm of our music, two cool cats, side by side.

Think Aloud

[3]*I notice the author uses the words* bippity bop *again at the end of the story. She also uses it in the title and as the sound of their secret knock. I think* bippity bop *is a happy sound to the characters in this story.*

After Reading

Retell the Story: Have children take turns retelling the beginning, middle, and end of the story.

Student Think Aloud

Use Copying Master number 1 to prompt children to share something they had a question about while listening to the story.

"I wonder . . ."

Think and Respond

1. What are some different feelings that Miles experiences in this story? *Possible responses: excitement, fear, confusion, happiness, pride* **Analytical**

2. How is this story different from a fable like "Anansi Saves Antelope"? *Possible responses: It doesn't have a lesson. It doesn't have animal characters. It is realistic.* **Genre**

3. Why do you think Natasha Tarpley wants you to read this story? *Possible responses: She wants me to compare my haircuts with the boy in the story. She wants to tell me how Miles feels when he gets his first haircut.* **Author's Purpose**

The Rooster and the Fox

an *Aesop* fable

retold by Madeline Juran

Genre: Fable

Comprehension Strategy: Draw Inferences

Think-Aloud Copying Master number 4

Before Reading

Genre: Tell children that you will be reading aloud a fable about two animals who are not normally friends. Remind children that fables are stories that teach a lesson. Ask children to explain the differences between a fable and a fairy tale.

Expand Vocabulary: Introduce these words before you begin reading the fable:

> *spotted:* saw
>
> *pleasant:* nice
>
> *errands:* short trips to do something
>
> *glance:* a quick look

Set a Purpose for Reading: Have children listen to find out if the Rooster and the Fox can become friends.

During Reading

Use the Think Alouds during the first reading of the story.

The Rooster and the Fox

an *Aesop* fable
retold by Madeline Juran

Genre Study

Fable: Animals often act like humans in fables. In this fable, the two animals talk and react to each other just like two people would.

One evening Rooster flew up into a tree to sleep. He fluffed his feathers and flapped his wings three times.

But just before he tucked his head under his wing, Rooster spotted a flash of red. It was moving behind the barn. He looked again and saw Fox standing beneath the tree.

"Good evening, Rooster," said Fox. "Have you heard the good news?"

Rooster was afraid of Fox, but he tried not to show it. "News?" he asked calmly. "What news?"

"Why, all the animals have agreed to love one another," said Fox.

"Oh, really?" said Rooster, trying to sound pleasant.

"That's right," said Fox. "From now on, we are all going to be friends. No more fighting, no more need to be afraid. We can all live together happily. Isn't that wonderful?"

"Hmmm. That is great news, Fox."

"Yes, so why don't you come down from that tree so I can give you a great big hug?"

But Rooster did not come down.[1] Instead, he stretched up on his tiptoes. He seemed to be looking at something far away.

"What are you looking at, Rooster?" asked Fox.

"I see the farmer's two dogs coming this way in a hurry," said Rooster. "Maybe they want to tell us—"

"Did you say dogs?" cried Fox. "So long, Rooster. I forgot—I have some important errands to take care of." And he turned to run away.[2]

"Wait!" cried Rooster. "Where are you going? The dogs are our friends now. Don't you want to give them a big hug, too?"

"No, thanks," Fox called back. "Maybe they haven't heard the good news yet." And off he ran across the pasture without a glance behind him.

Rooster chuckled. "A big hug indeed!" he said to himself. "I wouldn't trust Fox as far as I could throw the farmer's tractor."[3] Then he tucked his head under his wing and went to sleep.

Think Aloud

[1] I know that a fox will eat a rooster. I think that Rooster is being very smart by staying up in the tree. I am not sure if Fox can be trusted.

Think Aloud

[2] I figured out that Fox is not telling the truth because he runs away instead of waiting to give the dogs a big hug.

Think Aloud

[3] I was right! Rooster did not trust Fox all along. He was just playing along with Fox because he was scared of him. Smart Rooster!

After Reading

Retell the Story: Invite children to retell this fable with a partner.

Student Think Aloud

Use Copying Master number 4 to prompt children to share something that they figured out while listening to the fable.

"I figured out _____ because . . ."

Think and Respond

1. Who do you think is smarter: Rooster or Fox? Why? *Possible response: Rooster is smarter because he told Fox that two dogs were coming. He knew Fox was lying if Fox didn't want to meet the dogs.* **Critical**

2. How is this fable like other ones you have heard? *Possible responses: The fable has animal characters that behave as people do; it teaches a lesson.* **Genre**

3. What lesson do you think the author wants you to learn from this fable? *Possible responses: Be careful trusting someone who has always been mean to you. Don't always believe what you hear.* **Author's Purpose**

Trapped By Ice

by Ruth Musgrave

Genre: Nonfiction

Comprehension Strategy: Reread

Think-Aloud Copying Master number 6

Before Reading

Genre: Explain to children that the story you will be reading aloud is a true story about penguins that live in a very cold place called Antarctica. This story gives facts about the lives of the penguins and tells how they live in their cold environment. Remind children that they have heard other nonfiction selections such as "Tooth Tales From Around the World" and "Habitats: Where Animals Live."

Expand Vocabulary: Introduce the following words before reading the story:

> *iceberg:* a big, floating piece of ice broken from a glacier
>
> *chick:* a baby bird
>
> *hunt:* to search for
>
> *hatch:* to emerge from an egg

Set a Purpose for Reading: Ask children to listen to the story to find out something about penguins that they didn't know before.

During Reading

Use the Think Alouds during the first reading of the story. Notes about the genre and the cultural perspective may be used during subsequent readings.

Think Aloud

[1] *The iceberg hit the penguins' home. I wonder if the penguins will make it through the winter. If I keep listening, I think the author may tell me what happens to the penguins.*

Think Aloud

[2] *I thought the female penguin calling out to the male penguin was important because it tells me how she finds her mate. He must sound different to her than the other male penguins. This helps the penguins find each other in a big crowd. It also helps the female penguin get back to the nest in time for her chick to hatch.*

Trapped By Ice

by Ruth Musgrave

It all started in March 2000 when a huge iceberg broke off in Antarctica. In July 2001 a large piece of the iceberg crashed into an island where 1,200 male penguins were keeping their eggs warm. The female penguins were away looking for food at sea.[1]

The iceberg crushed the flat ice of the penguins' home. The cracked ice made it hard for the females to return to their nests. No eggs or chicks survived.

Gerald Kooyman, a penguin biologist watching what was happening in Antarctica, flew over nests in August 2002. "I was happy to see some adult penguins," he says. Still, he was afraid they would not make it through the winter. His next trip, in October (spring in Antarctica), made him feel better. He saw some parents and chicks and they were alive!

Every year as winter grows closer, almost 400,000 penguins leave the ocean and travel to places where they lay eggs and raise their chicks. Once there, each female lays one egg, gives it to the male penguin, and returns to sea to hunt for more food. It is now the male penguin's job to stand over the egg protecting it with his warm skin until it's ready to hatch.

The female penguin returns just before the chick hatches. To find her mate among the thousands of penguins that look alike, the female calls and he responds.[2]

Breaking away at its shell, the chick can take three days to hatch. As soon as the penguin hatches, the mom is there to feed it. The chick stays with the parent, until it is big enough to stay warm on its own.

Parents feed the baby chick food they get from the sea. At first, they take turns hunting and bringing food to the chick. Then both parents hunt, leaving the chick on its own for a while. The baby bird joins other chicks so that it can

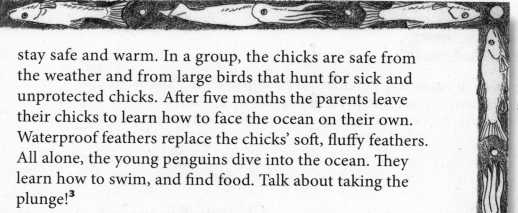

stay safe and warm. In a group, the chicks are safe from the weather and from large birds that hunt for sick and unprotected chicks. After five months the parents leave their chicks to learn how to face the ocean on their own. Waterproof feathers replace the chicks' soft, fluffy feathers. All alone, the young penguins dive into the ocean. They learn how to swim, and find food. Talk about taking the plunge![3]

Think Aloud

[3]The penguins dive into the ocean all alone. I wonder how they know what to do. I will listen to that part again. The author tells me that the parents leave their chicks and that the chicks' feathers become waterproof. So the chicks must be ready to be on their own now.

After Reading

Retell the Story: Write the heading "Penguins" at the top of a sheet of chart paper. Then have children tell facts about penguins that they learned from this story. Record their facts and read them aloud together when you are finished.

Student Think Aloud

Use Copying Master number 6 to prompt children to share something they found to be important in this story.

"I thought _____ was important because . . ."

Cultural Perspective

There are seventeen different kinds of penguins in the world. People from around the world work together to make sure that the penguins' homes are safe places for them to live.

Think and Respond

1. What is the most surprising or interesting thing you've learned about penguins? Why? *Responses will vary.* **Critical**

2. How do you know that this is not a make-believe story? *Possible response: There are many facts in the story that give real information about the lives of the penguins.* **Genre**

3. Why do you think the author wrote this story? *Possible response: She wanted to inform people about the lives of penguins and the dangers that they face.* **Author's Purpose**

What Is Made from Recycled Materials?

from *World Alamanac for Kids*

Genre: Reference

Comprehension Strategy: Generate Questions

Think-Aloud Copying Master number 1

 Before Reading

Genre: Tell children that a reference book has information that is arranged in an easy-to-understand way so we can get the facts we need. Reference books include dictionaries and encyclopedias.

Expand Vocabulary: Before reading, introduce these terms:

> *recycled:* put something through a special process so it is able to be used again
>
> *insulation:* material that keeps houses warm
>
> *steel:* a hard, strong metal
>
> *rubber:* a strong, stretchy material
>
> *speed bump:* raised bump on a road to prevent drivers from speeding

Set a Purpose for Reading: Tell children to think about things that they recycle at home and at school. Then tell them to listen to find out what kinds of items are made from these recycled materials.

 **During Reading**

Use the Think Alouds during the first reading of the selection. Notes about the genre and the cultural perspective may be used during subsequent readings.

Genre Study

Reference: The text is organized like a list. A list makes it easy to read and find information.

What Is Made from Recycled Materials?

- From <u>RECYCLED</u> PAPER we get newspapers, wrapping paper, cardboard containers, and <u>insulation</u>.

- From RECYCLED PLASTIC we get soda bottles, tables, benches, bicycle racks, cameras, backpacks, carpeting, shoes, and clothes.[1]

- From RECYCLED <u>STEEL</u> we get steel cans, cars, bicycles, nails, and refrigerators.

- From RECYCLED GLASS we get glass jars and tiles.

- From RECYCLED <u>RUBBER</u> we get bulletin boards, floor tiles, playground equipment, and speed bumps.[2]

Think Aloud

[1]*I wonder how the plastic milk carton that I recycle gets turned into something like a camera!*

Think Aloud

[2]*The author tells me information about recycling without a lot of extra sentences. This helps me quickly get just the facts I need.*

After Reading

Retell: Have children list one or two facts that they learned about recycling while listening to the selection. Then have children think of ways they can recycle at home.

Student Think Aloud

Use Copying Master number 1 to prompt children to share a question they have about this article.

"I wonder . . ."

Cultural Perspective

Earth Day is celebrated around the world on April 22 every year. The purpose of Earth Day is to remind people to take care of their home, Earth. Recycling things like paper, cans, and bottles is one easy way for everyone to help. Explain and discuss how recycling helps the Earth.

Think and Respond

1. Do you think it is important to recycle materials? Why or why not? *Possible response: Yes, it is important to recycle because we are helping our planet by reusing things.* **Critical**

2. How is this selection different from a story? *Possible responses: This selection is not make-believe. It gives information.* **Genre**

3. Why do you think the author wrote this selection? *Possible response: to make us aware of how important it is to recycle.* **Author's Purpose**

Joseph Had a Little Overcoat

a story
by Simms Taback

Genre: Fiction

Comprehension Strategy: Visualize

Think-Aloud Copying Master number 3

Before Reading

Genre: Remind children that a fiction story tells about something make-believe, or made up. Some stories, like the one you are about to read, are about things that could really happen. Help children remember other fiction stories they have heard, such as "We're Going on a Bear Hunt" or "Make Way for Ducklings."

Expand Vocabulary: Introduce these words before you read the story:

> *overcoat:* a heavy outer coat or jacket
>
> *handkerchief:* a small, square piece of cloth
>
> *suspenders:* a pair of elastic straps used to hold up pants

Set a Purpose for Reading: Have children listen to find out different ways that the main character, Joseph, reuses his overcoat.

During Reading

Use the Think Alouds during the first reading of the story. Notes about the genre and the cultural perspective may be used during subsequent readings.

Joseph Had a Little Overcoat

by Simms Taback

Joseph had a little <u>overcoat</u>. It was old and worn.
So he made a jacket out of it
and went to the fair.

Joseph had a little jacket. It got old and worn.
So he made a vest out of it
and danced at his nephew's wedding.

Joseph had a little vest. It got old and worn.[1]
So he made a scarf out of it
and sang in the men's chorus.

Joseph had a little scarf. It got old and worn.
So he made a necktie out of it
and went to visit his married sister in the city.

Joseph had a little necktie. It got old and worn.
So he made a <u>handkerchief</u> out of it
and drank a glass of hot tea with lemon.

Joseph had a little handkerchief. It got old and worn.
So he made a button out of it
and used it to fasten his <u>suspenders</u>.[2]

Joseph had a little button. One day he lost it.
Now he had nothing.

So Joseph made a book about it. Which shows . . .
you can always make something out of nothing.

Retell the Story: Have children make a drawing of Joseph wearing something he made from his little overcoat. Invite them to take turns describing the clothing in their pictures.

Student Think Aloud

Use Copying Master number 3 to prompt children to share what they visualized while listening to this story.

"I was able to picture in my mind . . ."

Cultural Perspective

This award-winning story is based on an old Jewish folk song from Eastern Europe.

Think and Respond

1. What else might Joseph do with his little overcoat when it gets old and worn? *Possible responses: He could put it on a scarecrow. He could give it to someone who did not have a coat.* **Critical**

2. Do you think this story could really happen? Why? *Possible response: Yes, a person really could cut down a coat into other things; a person could go to all the places Joseph did.* **Genre**

3. What do you think the author means by the last line of the story, "you can always make something out of nothing"? *Possible response: If you use your imagination, you can get by without having a lot of things.* **Author's Purpose**

The Power of Weather

from *Scholastic News*

Genre: Nonfiction

Comprehension Strategy: Use Text Structure

Think-Aloud Copying Master number 5

Before Reading

Genre: Remind children that nonfiction selections tell information about different subjects. Tell them that the next selection they will hear gives facts about different types of weather. Suggest that children think about other nonfiction stories they have heard, such as "Tooth Tales From Around the World."

Expand Vocabulary: Introduce the following words before reading this selection:

>*weather:* the condition of the air around us
>
>*harmful:* capable of doing damage
>
>*panels:* flat sections

Set a Purpose for Reading: As you read, have children listen for good and bad things about rain, wind, and the sun.

During Reading

Use the Think Alouds during the first reading of the story. Notes about the genre and the cultural perspective may be used during subsequent readings.

The Power of Weather

<u>Weather</u> is powerful! It can help and harm all living things.

Helpful Rain

Rain gives plants water to drink. First, rain sinks into the ground. Then, plants suck up the rainwater through their roots. What else needs water to live?

<u>Harmful</u> Rain

Too much rain can cause a flood. Most floods happen when rain makes a river too full. The water spills into streets, cars, homes, and stores.

Helpful Wind

Wind helps spread seeds. It blows seeds to new places. Later, the seeds grow into new plants.

Harmful Wind[1]

Wind can make a dangerous storm! A tornado is a kind of storm. Its winds spin around and around. A tornado's winds are so strong that they can rip trees out of the ground!

Helpful Sun

The sun helps warm some homes. <u>Panels</u> on the roof trap the sun's heat. This heat is used to warm the home's air. It also warms water for the bath and shower.

Harmful Sun

The sun can also cause a sunburn. Ouch! People must use sunscreen to protect their skin. Then, they can enjoy a sunny day!

Think! What else besides sunscreen do people use to protect themselves from the weather?[2]

Think Aloud

[1]*I noticed the author used the words* helpful *and* harmful *before each kind of weather. This helps me understand what I will be hearing and it helps me predict what I will learn about in each section.*

Think Aloud

[2]*I've seen a lot of people wearing hats when they go out in the sun. A baseball cap can help protect your head.*

After Reading

Retell: Have children fold a sheet of drawing paper in half. On one half, have them draw a picture of how weather can be helpful. On the other half, have them draw a picture of how weather can be harmful. Allow time for them to explain what they have drawn.

Student Think Aloud

Use Copying Master number 5 to prompt children to share something that they noticed the author did in presenting the information.

"I noticed the author . . ."

Cultural Perspective

One of the hottest temperatures ever recorded was in the country of Libya in 1922. The temperature rose to 136° F.

Think and Respond

1. How has weather been helpful for you? How has it been harmful? *Responses will vary.* **Analytical**

2. How do you know that this is a nonfiction selection? *Possible responses: the selection tells facts about weather; the information is true; it's not a make-believe story.* **Genre**

3. What point do you think the author tries to make with this selection? *Possible responses: Weather is powerful. Most of the time we can live with it, but sometimes it changes our lives.* **Author's Purpose**

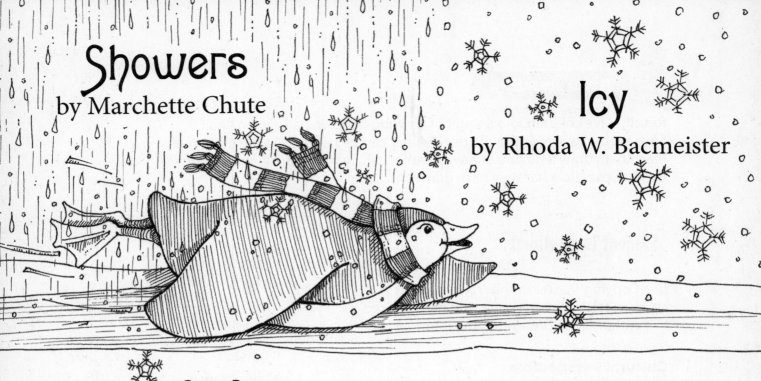

Showers
by Marchette Chute

Icy
by Rhoda W. Bacmeister

Genre: Poem

Poetic Element: Alliteration

Comprehension Strategy: Visualize

Think-Aloud Copying Master number 3

Before Reading

Genre: Tell children that the poems they will listen to describe what rain sounds like and what it feels like to move on ice. Tell children that poets paint a picture of something by using just a few interesting and unusual words. Some poems use alliteration or words beginning with the same sound.

Expand Vocabulary: Before reading these two poems, introduce these words:

squelch: to crush, smash, or squeeze

skid: to slide out of control

crust: a crisp outer layer

Set a Purpose for Reading: As children listen to the poems, tell them to close their eyes and focus on what rain sounds like and how snow and ice feel. Have them listen for alliteration.

During Reading

Read through the poems the first time without interruptions, using an expressive tone to emphasize the alliteration. The Think Aloud and genre note may be used during subsequent readings.

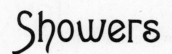

Showers

by Marchette Chute

Squelch and squirt and squiggle,
Drizzle and drip and drain—
Such a lot of water
Comes down with the rain![1]

Icy

by Rhoda W. Bacmeister

I slip and I slide
On the slippery ice;
I skid and I glide—
Oh, isn't it nice
To lie on your tummy
And slither and skim
On the slick crust of snow
Where you skid as you swim?

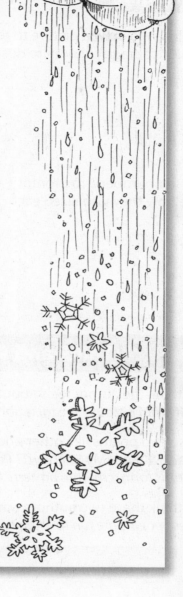

Think Aloud

[1] *I was able to picture in my mind a rainy day with drops dripping off everything because of all those describing words in the poem.*

Genre Study

Alliteration: Alliteration, the repetition of consonant sounds usually at the beginning of words, is often used in poems. Saying the same sounds several times makes the reader focus more on the words he or she is reading.

After Reading

Retell: Invite children to draw a picture to retell the rain poem, and one for the icy poem. Encourage children to describe their drawings using alliteration.

Student Think Aloud

Use Copying Master number 3 to prompt children to share how they visualized each poem.

"I was able to picture in my mind . . ."

Think and Respond

1. How do you think the author feels about ice? Why? *Possible response: She likes it and thinks it is fun because she talks about sliding and playing on it.* **Analytical**

2. How are these two poems like other poems you have listened to such as "Hide and Seek Shadow" and "My Shadow"? *Possible responses: They all have rhyming words. The words form a rhythm pattern.* **Genre**

3. Why do you think these two authors want you to read these poems? *Possible response: These poems are fun to listen to and read aloud.* **Author's Purpose**

Digging For Clues

by Kate Duke

Genre: Informational Fiction

Text Structure: Description

Comprehension Strategy: Summarize

Think-Aloud Copying Master number 7

 Before Reading

Genre: Explain that informational fiction gives factual information but also tells a story. Point out that this selection will give information about a science called archaeology while telling a made-up story about characters who experience a "dig" first-hand.

Expand Vocabulary: Introduce these words before you read the story:

treasure: something of great worth or value

ordinary: the regular condition or course of things

tool: a handheld device that helps perform a task

clue: something that helps a person find something or solve a mystery

Set a Purpose for Reading: Have children listen to find out what archaeologists are interested in and why.

 **During Reading**

Then use the Think Alouds during the first reading of the story. Notes about the genre and the cultural perspective may be used during subsequent readings.

Digging For Clues

by Kate Duke

As this story begins, some children are getting ready to help their friend Sophie. Sophie is an archaeologist. An archaeologist is a scientist who studies how people lived a long time ago. One way archaeologists learn is by carefully digging up places where people lived long ago. Sophie tells the children that they are going to do some digging. This is how archaeologists dig—neat and organized.

This dig is happening at a place where people lived thousands of years ago. They lived by hunting, but we don't know much more about them. Let's see what the children find.

We couldn't wait to do a little digging ourselves. Maybe we'd find some treasure! Maybe we'd find some gold! Or a mummy![1]

But when we looked at the stuff Sophie had already found, we were confused. It just looked like a bunch of rocks and pebbles and dirt. It sure didn't look like treasure.

That was when we learned the truth about archaeology.

The truth was a shock. Archaeologists hardly ever find treasure. They aren't even trying to! They look for ordinary things that belonged to ordinary people. They even care about the stuff that people dropped, lost, or threw away. In other words, garbage. Archaeologists love old garbage!

When they study it and test it, they can find out all kinds of things about the people it once belonged to.[2] So archaeologists are more like detectives than treasure hunters. They're trying to find the whole story of how people used to live.

So Sophie's dirt wasn't just dirt. It had bits of six-thousand-year-old garbage in it. There were little pieces of bones and shells. They showed what animals the people hunted long ago. And even littler pieces of black charcoal showed what plants they ate. Those pieces once had been seeds and nutshells. They had fallen into the fire and burned while being cooked for somebody's dinner, one day thousands of years ago.

Think Aloud

[1] I think that being an archaeologist is exciting. You never know what you are going to find!

Think Aloud

[2] At first I thought that archaeologists only find treasures, but then I found out that treasures are rarely found. Archaeologists can learn a lot from ordinary objects.

Sophie's rocks weren't just rocks, either. They were things that people made. Someone had turned those rocks into something important by using them everyday.

They are <u>clues</u> to the past. And like detectives at a crime scene, when archaeologists dig, they try not to break anything that might be a clue. They use <u>tools</u> that can dig gently. And they never ever take anything away from the dig without first marking down exactly where it came from. Knowing where something was found can help explain why it was there and what it was used for.

Finally we were ready to start digging. Sophie gave us each a teeny little tool to work with. No shovels! She told us to scrape the dirt up lightly, taking off only the tiniest bit at a time.

After that, we learned how to look through the dirt we'd gathered, to be sure we hadn't missed anything tiny. We worked for hours and got really hot and sweaty. Then, finally, we found our first clue.

It was an awl. An awl is like a needle without the hole at one end. A person had probably used it long ago to sew pieces of leather into clothes.

We held it in our hands and thought about how no one had touched it for all those years, until now.[3]

Genre Study

Informational Fiction: This selection uses made-up characters to show the special way that archaeologists dig for clues. Informational fiction mixes fiction with facts.

Think Aloud

[3]*This was mostly about archaeologists and how the clues they dig for can teach us about people who lived a long time ago.*

After Reading

Retell the Story: Have children pretend that they are on the "dig" with Sophie and take a picture of something from the dig with their camera. Ask children to "draw" their photograph on a piece of 5" x 7" paper. Place the "photos" in a simple album and have children look through the pictures and tell what is happening in each of them.

Student Think Aloud

Use Copying Master number 7 to prompt children to share something that they learned from listening to this story.

"This story was mostly about . . ."

Cultural Perspective

Nearly 2,000 years ago, the city of Pompeii, Italy, was buried under lava and ash when a volcano erupted. Archaeologists have spent hundreds of years uncovering clues at this site that tell them how people lived long ago.

Think and Respond

1. What do you think is the best part about being an archaeologist? *Responses will vary. Possible responses: I think finding things from long ago is the best part.* **Critical**

2. Identify ways that the author mixes her imagination with facts in this story. *Possible responses: She tells about the experiences of made-up characters like Sophie and the person telling the story. But she also includes real information about what an archaeologist does.* **Genre**

3. What do you think the author wants you to know about the work of archaeologists? *Possible response: Archaeology is hard work. There is more to it than just digging for things in the dirt.* **Author's Purpose**

What Kind of Scientist Are You?

from *Fun for Kidz*

Genre: Nonfiction

Comprehension Strategy: Summarize

Think-Aloud Copying Master number 7

Before Reading

Genre: Remind children that nonfiction articles give information. Remind children of other nonfiction selections they have heard, such as "The Power of Weather."

Expand Vocabulary: Introduce the following words before you begin reading:

> *composition:* what something is made of
>
> *earthquakes:* movements of the ground that feel like strong shaking
>
> *human behavior:* the way people act

Set a Purpose for Reading: Have children listen to learn about different kinds of scientists.

During Reading

Use the Think Alouds during the first reading of the story. Notes about the genre and cultural perspective may be used during subsequent readings.

What Kind of Scientist Are You?

There are many different kinds of science. Some sciences help us understand the human body. Others teach us about the sun and the planets. Listen as I read this information about scientists. A scientist is a person who studies and knows a lot about a type of science.

Genre Study

Nonfiction: Since nonfiction stories have a lot of information, listing the facts can help us better understand what the author is communicating.

We all know what an astronomer is. An astronomer is a scientist who studies the planets and the stars. An oceanographer is a scientist who studies the oceans. Both of those words end in the letters "er." The names of most scientists end in the letters "ist," just like in the word "scientist." A chemist is a scientist who studies the composition of things. A biologist is a scientist who studies living plants and animals. Those words end in the letters "ist." Astronomer, oceanographer, chemist, and biologist are all titles of scientists that you are probably familiar with.[1] Below, we have listed several more. Some you will have heard of, but we think some will be new to you.

- A herpetologist is a scientist who studies snakes.
- A vulcanologist is a scientist who studies volcanoes.
- An entomologist is a scientist who studies insects.
- An ichthyologist is a scientist who studies fishes.
- A paleontologist is a scientist who studies prehistoric life.
- A seismologist is a scientist who studies earthquakes and movement of the surface of the earth.
- An ornithologist is a scientist who studies birds.
- An ophthalmologist is a scientist who studies eyes.
- A geologist is a scientist who studies the origin, history, and structure of the earth.
- An ecologist is a scientist who studies the relationship between living things and the environment.
- A meteorologist is a scientist who studies the weather.
- A psychologist is a scientist who studies human behavior.[2]

Think Aloud

[1] *At first I thought that there were only a few kinds of scientists, and then I found out that there are so many.*

Think Aloud

[2] *This was mostly about all the different kinds of scientists there are, and what they do.*

 **After Reading**

Retell: Have children list one or two facts that they learned about scientists while listening to the selection.

Student Think Aloud

Use Copying Master number 7 to prompt children to summarize the selection.

"This story was mostly about . . ."

Cultural Perspective

A scientist who studies human beings, the way they live, and their beliefs is called an *anthropologist*. They may travel across the world to study new and old cultures.

Think and Respond

1. What kind of scientist would you like to be? Why? *Responses will vary.* **Critical**

2. How is this selection similar to the reference selection you heard, "What Is Made from Recycled Materials?" *Possible responses: It lists information. It organizes information so it is easy to find.* **Text Structure**

3. Why do you think the author wrote this selection? *Possible response: to teach us about all the different kinds of scientists there are and about the work they do.* **Author's Purpose**

The Gingerbread Man

a folk tale
edited by Nicola Baxter

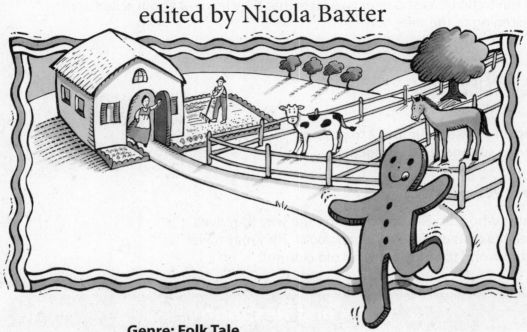

Genre: Folk Tale

Comprehension Strategy: Summarize

Think-Aloud Copying Master number 1

Before Reading

Genre: Explain that "The Gingerbread Man" is a folk tale that has been told over and over again. It is a story that has been passed down through generations. This folk tale is called a "runaway story" because the main character is trying to run away from its creator.

Expand Vocabulary: Before reading, introduce these terms:

   faint: weak

   assistance: help

   gratefully: thankfully

   pursuers: people or animals chasing someone or something

Set a Purpose for Reading: Have children listen to find out if anyone can catch the gingerbread man.

During Reading

Use the Think Alouds during the first reading of the story. Notes about the genre and cultural perspective may be used during subsequent readings.

The Gingerbread Man

Once upon a time a little old man and a little old woman lived in a cottage in the country. One day, the little old woman made some ginger cookies. When she had rolled out the dough and cut out two trays of cookies, she still had some left over.

"I will make a little gingerbread man," she said to herself, "as a surprise for my husband."

So she cut out the shape of a gingerbread man. She gave him three buttons and two eyes made of raisins and a smiley mouth made out of a cherry. Then she put him in the oven with the other cookies.

Soon the delicious smell of baking cookies filled the kitchen. But when the little old woman went to take them out of the oven, she thought she heard a <u>faint</u> voice inside. She opened the oven door and almost fell over with surprise. The little gingerbread man jumped up from the tray and ran toward the kitchen door, as fast as his legs would carry him.[1]

"Come back!" shouted the little old woman, running after him.

"Come back!" shouted the little old man, who was working in the garden.

They both ran after the gingerbread man. But the bold gingerbread man called over his shoulder. "Run, run, as fast as you can! You can't catch me, I'm the gingerbread man!"

The gingerbread man ran down the garden path and out onto the road. As he ran he passed a cow in a field.

"Stop!" mooed the cow. "You look much nicer to eat than this grass." And she ran after the little man.

But the gingerbread man didn't stop for a second. "A little old woman and a little old man couldn't catch me and neither will you! Run, run, as fast as you can! You won't catch me, I'm the gingerbread man!" he called out.

In the next field he passed a horse. "Stop!" neighed the horse. "You look much nicer to eat than this hay."

But the gingerbread man kept running. "A little old woman and a little old man and a cow couldn't catch me and neither will you! Run, run, as fast as you can! You won't catch me, I'm the gingerbread man!" he shouted.

A rooster sitting on a gate saw the gingerbread man. "Stop!" he cock-a-doodle-dooed. "You look much nicer to eat than this grain." And he flapped after the gingerbread man.

Think Aloud

[1]*I wonder where the little gingerbread man is going. I will listen to see.*

Genre Study

Folk Tale: Many folk tales have a pattern in which events are repeated again and again by different characters. Repetition supports an idea and makes it clearer to the reader.

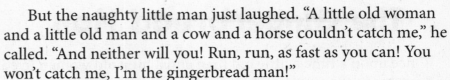

But the naughty little man just laughed. "A little old woman and a little old man and a cow and a horse couldn't catch me," he called. "And neither will you! Run, run, as fast as you can! You won't catch me, I'm the gingerbread man!"

Just then the gingerbread man passed a pig in a yard. "Stop!" grunted the pig. "You look much nicer to eat than this slop."

The gingerbread man ran even faster. "A little old woman and a little old man and a cow and a horse and a rooster couldn't catch me," he called. "And neither will you!"

But at the end of the next field, the little man came to a wide river and there he had to stop. For although gingerbread men are very good at running, they don't know how to swim at all.

"Can I help you?" asked a quiet voice nearby. It was a big red fox. "Perhaps you need some <u>assistance</u> in crossing the river? Pray allow me to help. Just jump on my back and I will carry you across."[2]

The gingerbread man <u>gratefully</u> did as the fox said, for his <u>pursuers</u> were coming closer and closer. Without hesitating the fox swam into the fast flowing river.

But soon the fox spoke again. "The water is getting deeper. Climb onto my head and you will stay dry." And the gingerbread man did so.

"The water is even deeper here," said the fox. "Climb onto my nose and you will stay dry."

No sooner had the gingerbread man climbed onto the fox's nose when the fox smiled a wide smile. He threw up his head and the gingerbread man flew up into the air. Then down he fell, right into the fox's open mouth.[3]

Pretty soon the little old woman and the little old man and the cow and the horse and the rooster and the pig came puffing up to the bank of the river. The gingerbread man was nowhere to be seen. But in the middle of the river, a duck pecked at a few last crumbs floating on the water.

Think Aloud

[2]*I know that in some stories a fox is an animal that you cannot trust. This fox certainly talks like a nice fox. Maybe this story will be different, but the gingerbread man had better be careful.*

Think Aloud

[3]*I was right! The fox could not be trusted even when he seemed so helpful. I think this story is like a fable. It teaches a lesson about trust.*

After Reading

Retell: Have children retell the story by acting it out. Assign roles of the man, woman, gingerbread man, cow, horse, pig, and fox.

Student Think Aloud

Use Copying Master number 1 to prompt children to share a question they had while listening to this story.

"I wonder . . ."

Cultural Perspective

Gingerbread has been baked in Europe for hundreds of years. It can be made to look like dark squares of bread or shaped like people.

Think and Respond

1. What words would you use to describe the gingerbread man? Why? *Possible response: naughty, proud, very sure of himself; He thought he was faster and better than everyone else.* **Analytical**

2. Name some places where words and actions are repeated in this story. *Possible responses: The gingerbread man repeats the same line. The animals all tell him to stop because he looks so good to eat.* **Genre**

3. Why do you think this story has been told over and over again? *Possible responses: It is a fun story to picture in your mind. It has a surprise ending. It teaches a lesson about trust.* **Author's Purpose**

THE BOY WHO CRIED "WOLF"

an *Aesop* fable

Genre: Fable

Comprehension Strategy: Summarize

Think-Aloud Copying Master number 7

Before Reading

Genre: Tell children that you will be reading another fable that teaches a lesson by the author named Aesop. Discuss other Aesop fables children are familiar with, such as "The Rooster and the Fox" and "The Tortoise and the Hare."

Expand Vocabulary: Introduce these words before you read this fable:

> *honesty:* the ability to tell the truth
>
> *shepherd:* a person who watches over sheep
>
> *flock:* a group of sheep
>
> *fold:* a group

Set a Purpose for Reading: Tell children that the lesson taught in this fable is the first line of the story. Ask them to think about this lesson as they listen to the rest of the story.

During Reading

Use the Think Alouds during the first reading of the story. The genre study may be used during subsequent readings.

THE BOY WHO CRIED "WOLF"

an *Aesop* fable

The fastest way to lose what we call our good character is to lose our honesty.

There was once a shepherd boy who kept his flock at a little distance from the village. Once he thought he would play a trick on the villagers and have some fun at their expense.[1] So he ran toward the village crying out, with all his might: "Wolf! Wolf! Come and help! The wolves are at my lambs!"

The kind villagers left their work and ran to the field to help him. But when they got there the boy laughed at them for their pains; there was no wolf there.

Still another day the boy tried the same trick, and the villagers came running to help and were laughed at again.

Then one day a wolf did break into the fold and began killing the lambs. In great fright, the boy ran back for help. "Wolf! Wolf!" he screamed. "There is a wolf in the flock! Help!"

The villagers heard him, but they thought it was another mean trick; no one paid the least attention, or went near him. And the shepherd boy lost all his sheep.[2]

That is the kind of thing that happens to people who lie: even when they do tell the truth they will not be believed.

After Reading

Retell the Story: Have children retell the story by acting it out. Assign roles of the boy, wolf, sheep, and villagers.

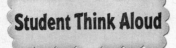

Use Copying Master number 7 to prompt children to summarize the story.

"This story was mostly about . . ."

Think and Respond

1. What do you think the boy learned from this experience? *Possible response: to always tell the truth* **Inferential**

2. How is this fable different from others you have heard? *Possible response: It has human characters instead of animal characters.* **Genre**

3. Why do you think the author wrote this fable? *Possible response: to teach us not to play tricks on others; to warn us to be honest with others* **Author's Purpose**

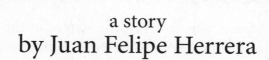

a story
by Juan Felipe Herrera

Genre: Realistic Fiction

Comprehension Strategy: Visualize

Think-Aloud Copying Master number 3

 Before Reading

Genre: Remind children that realistic fiction tells about things that could really happen. Explain to children that the author of this realistic fiction story is remembering events that happened to him as a child. He has created characters and events out of his memories. Invite children to recall other realistic fiction stories, such as "Bippity Bop Barbershop."

Expand Vocabulary: Explain to children that there are many Spanish words used in the story. Introduce these words before you begin reading:

> *campesinos:* the Spanish word for "field workers"
>
> *chico:* the Spanish word for "boy"
>
> *Buenos dias:* the Spanish phrase for "good morning"
>
> *harmonica:* a small musical instrument played by blowing in and out

Set a Purpose for Reading: Have children listen in order to picture the story in their minds.

 **During Reading**

Use the Think Alouds during the first reading of the story. Notes about the genre and the cultural perspective may be used during subsequent readings.

Think Aloud

[1] *I can figure out why the characters are calling the street Who-nee-purr. The family pronounces the word Juniper like Who-nee-purr. That is because they speak Spanish and are just learning to speak English.*

THE UPSIDE DOWN BOY

by Juan Felipe Herrera

When I was little, my family spent years working in the fields as campesinos. One day, my mama said to my papi, "Let's settle down. It's time that Juanito goes to school." That year we were living in the mountains by Lake Wolfer, a glassy world full of sky colors.

Papi's old army truck brought us down the steep mountain roads, all the way to Mrs. Andasola's pink house on Juniper Street. I was eight years old and about to live in a big city for the first time.

— Juan Felipe Herrera

Mama, who loves words, sings out the name on the street sign—Juniper. "Who-nee-purr! Who-nee-purr!"[1]

Papi parks our old army truck on Juniper Street in front of Mrs. Andasola's tiny pink house. "We found it at last," Papi shouts, "Who-nee-purr!"

"Time to start school," Mama tells me with music in her voice. "My Who-nee-purr Street!" I yell to the chickens in the yard.

"Don't worry, *chico*," Papi says as he walks me to school. "Everything changes. A new place has new leaves on the trees and blows fresh air into your body."

I pinch my ear. Am I really here? Maybe the street lamp is really a golden cornstalk with a dusty gray coat.

People speed by alone in their fancy melting cars. In the valleys, campesinos sang "*Buenos dias, Juanito.*"

I make a clown face, half funny, half scared. "I don't speak English," I say to Papi. "Will my tongue turn into a rock?"

I slow step into school. My *burrito de papas*, my potato burrito in a brown bag. Empty playground, fences locked. One cloud up high.

No one in the halls. Open a door with a blue number 27. "*¿Donde estoy?*" Where am I? My question in Spanish fades as the thick door slams behind me.

Mrs. Sampson, the teacher, shows me my desk. Kids laugh when I poke my nose into my lunch bag.

The hard round clock above my head clicks and aims its strange arrows at me.

On the chalkboard, I see a row of alphabet letters and addition numbers. If I learn them will they grow like seeds?

If I learn the English words will my voice reach the ceiling, weave through it like grape vines?

We are finger-painting. I make wild suns with my open hands. Crazy tomato cars and cucumber sombreros—I write my name with seven chiles.

"What is that?" Mrs. Sampson asks. My tongue is a rock.[2]

The school bell rings and shakes me.

I run and grab my lunch bag and sit on the green steel bench. In a few fast minutes, I finish my potato burrito. But everyone plays, and I am alone.

"It is only recess," my classmate Amanda says in Spanish. In Spanish, I pronounce "recess" slowly. "Sounds like 'reses'—like the word for cattle, huh?" I say.

"What is recess?" I ask Amanda.

The high bell roars again. This time everyone eats their sandwiches while I play in the breezy baseball diamond by myself.

"Is this recess?" I ask again.

When I jump up everyone sits. When I sit all the kids swing through the air. My feet float through the clouds when all I want is to touch the earth. I am the upside down boy.[3]

Papi comes home to Mrs. Andasola's pink house. I show him my finger painting. "What a spicy sun," he sings out. "It reminds me of hot summer days in the San Joaquin Valley," he says, brushing his dark hair with his hands.

"Look, mama! See my painting?"

"Those are flying tomatoes ready for salsa," Mama sings. She shows my painting to Mrs. Andasola who shows it to Gabino, her canary.

"Gabino, Gabino, see?" Mrs. Andasola yells. "What do you think?" Gabino nods his head back and forth. "Pío, pío, piiiii!"

Mrs. Sampson invites me to the front of the class. "Sing, Juanito, sing a song we have been practicing."

I pop up shaking. I am alone facing the class.

"Ready to sing?" Mrs. Sampson asks me. I am frozen, then a deep breath fills me, "Three blind mice, three blind mice," I sing.

My eyes open as big as the ceiling and my hands spread out as if catching rain drops from the sky.

"You have a very beautiful voice, Juanito," Mrs. Sampson says. "What is beautiful?" I ask Amanda after school.

Think Aloud

[2]*Juanito says his tongue is a rock. I think that means it feels heavy in his mouth. He is afraid to speak because he doesn't speak English very well. I can understand how he feels when he says this.*

Think Aloud

[3]*I was able to picture in my mind what happened to Juanito at recess. How sad he must have looked eating lunch all by himself while the other kids played. And he must have looked very lonely and small on the baseball diamond. I can see now why he calls himself the upside down boy. He feels different from everyone else.*

At home, I help Mama and Mrs. Andasola make *buñuelos*—fried sweet cinnamon tortilla chips.

"Piiiiicho, come heeeere," I sing out, calling my dog as I stretch a dough ball.

"Listen to meeeee," I sing to Picho with his ears curled up into fuzzy triangles. "My voice is beauuuuutiful!"

"What is he singing?" Mrs. Andasola asks my mom as she gently lays a buñuelo into the frying pan.

"My teacher says my voice is beauuuuutiful," I sing, dancing with a tiny dough ball stuck on my nose.

"*Sí, sí*," Mama laughs. "Let's see if your buñuelos come out beautiful too."

"I only made it to the third grade, Juanito," Mama tells me as I get ready for bed.

"When we lived in El Paso, Texas, my mother needed help at home. We were very poor and she was tired from cleaning people's houses."

"That year your mama won a spelling medal," Papi says as he shaves in the bathroom.

"Your Papi learned English without a school," Mama says. "When he worked the railroads, he would pay his buddies a penny for each word they taught him."

Papi says softly, "Each word, each language has its own magic."

After a week of reading a new poem aloud to us every day Mrs. Sampson says, "Write a poem," as she plays symphony music on the old red phonograph.

I think of Mama, squeeze my pencil, pour letters from the shiny tip like a skinny river. The waves tumble onto the page. L's curl at the bottom. F's tip their hats from their heads. M's are sea waves. They crash over my table.

Juanito's Poem

Papi Felipe with a mustache of words.
Mama Lucha with strawberries in her hair.
I see magic salsa in my house and everywhere!

"I got an A on my poem!" I yell to everyone in the front yard where Mama gives Papi a haircut.

I show Gabino my paper as I fly through the kitchen to the backyard.

"Listen," I sing to the baby chicks, with my hands up as if I am a famous music conductor.

I sprinkle corn kernels and sing out my poem. Each fuzzy chick gets a name:

"Beethoven! You are the one with the bushy head!
Mozart! You jumpy black-spotted hen!
Johann Sebastian! Tiny red rooster, dance, dance!"

In the morning, as we walk to school Papi turns and says, "You do have a nice voice, Juanito. I never heard you sing until yesterday when you fed the chickens. At first, when we moved here, you looked sad and I didn't know what to do."

"I felt funny, upside down," I say to him. "The city streets aren't soft with flowers. Buildings don't have faces. You know, Papi, in the campo I knew all the names, even of those bugs with little wild eyes and shiny noses!"

"Here," he says. "Here's my harmonica. It has many voices, many beautiful songs just like you. Sing them!"

On Open House Day, Mama and Papi sit in the front row. Mrs. Andasola admires our drawings on the walls, Gabino on her shoulder.

"Our paintings look like the flowery fields back in the Valley," I tell Amanda.

"I have a surprise," I whisper to Mama. "I am '*El Maestro Juanito*,' the choir conductor!" Mrs. Sampson smiles wearing a chile sombrero and puts on the music.

I blow a "C" with my harmonica—"La la la laaaaah! Ready to sing out your poems?" I ask my choir. "*Uno . . . dos . . .* and three!"

After Reading

Retell the Story: Have children draw a picture to show something that happened in the story. Have them use their pictures to retell the story.

Student Think Aloud

Use Copying Master number 3 to prompt children to share how they pictured an event or character in their minds.

"I can picture in my mind . . ."

Cultural Perspective

The author Juan Felipe Herrera is a Mexican American poet. His parents were migrant farm workers who traveled throughout California's San Joaquin Valley picking fruits and vegetables to earn money. Herrera is also a musician, an actor, and a college teacher.

Discuss with children how the author's background and cultural traditions influenced his writing. Help children recognize that the values, beliefs, and interests of an author are reflected in literature. Encourage children to respect the ages, genders, and cultural traditions of the various authors they study.

Think and Respond

1. Why do you think Juanito feels like he is upside down in this story? Do you think he feels this way at the end? *Possible response: He feels like he is doing everything at the opposite time as his classmates. No, I don't think he feels this way at the end.* **Inferential**

2. How is the story like other realistic fiction stories you have heard? *Possible response: It tells about people and things that could really be true.* **Genre**

3. What does the author want you to learn about moving to a new place? *Possible response: Moving to a new place can be scary, especially if you speak a different language.* **Author's Purpose**

Hilda Must Be Dancing

a story
by Karma Wilson

Genre: Fantasy

Comprehension Strategy: Visualize

Think-Aloud Copying Master number 3

Before Reading

Genre: Remind children that a fantasy is a story that blends make-believe things with things that could be true. Explain that in this fantasy the characters do realistic things like talk and dance, but they are all animals. Ask children to recall another fantasy that they have heard, "Beverly Billingsly Borrows a Book."

Expand Vocabulary: Before reading, introduce these terms:

> *leotard:* a stretchy outfit worn by a dancer
>
> *pirouette:* a ballet motion that involves twirling the body around
>
> *wallowed:* rolled around
>
> *encore:* a French word that an audience calls out when they want a performer to repeat the performance

Set a Purpose for Reading: Have children listen in order to picture the dancing hippo in their minds.

During Reading

Use the Think Alouds during the first reading of the story. Notes about the genre and the cultural perspective may be used during subsequent readings.

Hilda Must Be Dancing

by Karma Wilson

Hilda Hippo loved to dance,
and so each day she practiced hard.
She'd twist and turn and whirl and twirl,
dressed in her favorite leotard.

She'd spin a pretty pirouette,
then leap and land on tippy-toe.

She tangoed oh-so-gracefully,
and square-danced with a do-si-do.

And while she danced in utter bliss,
it sounded quite a lot like this:
KA-BUMP! KA-BUMP!
CRASH! CRASH! SMASH!
THUMPITY-BUMP!
THUMPITY-BUMP!
BOOM! BANG! BASH!

The jungle floor would
shake and quake,
a tidal wave would
fill the lake.
Her friends would shout,
"For goodness' sake,
Hilda must be dancing!"

They all hoped Hilda's hobby
was a stage that soon would pass.
But after one loud, shaky year,
they knew this phase would last . . .
    and last . . .
        and last.

When Hilda danced flamenco
in her favorite pair of heels,
bananas fell in gooey heaps,
shaken from their peels!
SWISHA-SWISHA CLAP! CLAP!
JUMP, JUMP, JUMP!

"Hilda must be dancing!"
cried the monkeys from the trees.
"Perhaps she'd take up knitting
if we asked her, pretty please?"[1]

Hilda tried to
sit and knit.
She didn't like it,
not one bit.

The yarn got tangled,
so she quit.
"I think I'll stick to dancing."

She rumbaed and she sambaed
in her favorite flowered skirt.
She skipped across the crowded plains
and kicked up clouds of dirt.
HIPPA-HIPPA
BOUNCE! BOUNCE!
THUMP, THUMP, THUMP![2]

"Hilda must be dancing!"
said the rhinos in distress.
"If she'd only take up singing,
then she wouldn't make a mess!"

Hilda tried to
hum and croon,
but found she couldn't
hold a tune.

She tired of it
very soon.
"I think I'll stick to dancing!"

At the water hole she boogied
in her favorite disco pants.
She muddied up the river
and she trampled
down the plants.
SHAKA-SHAKA
BOOM! BOOM!
BUMP, BUMP, BUMP!

Think Aloud

[1]As I am listening, I hear rhyming words. I figure out that this story is written like a poem.

Think Aloud

[2]I was able to picture in my mind the big mess Hilda makes as she stomps around kicking up dirt. A big hippo like Hilda must look very silly dancing in a skirt!

"Hilda must be dancing!"
wailed the water buffalo.
"If she'd only take up swimming,
we might get some peace, you know?"

And so . . .
Hilda wallowed
by the shore.
She'd never felt
so grand before!
"Now, here's a hobby
I adore. . . .
"Water ballet dancing!"

In her favorite two-piece suit
she whirled and twirled with flair.
Best of all, the ground stayed still!
She floated light as air.

And while she swam and danced in bliss,
it sounded quite a lot like this:
KER-PLOP! KER-PLOP!
PLUNK! DUNK! SWISH!
GLUBBITY-GLUB! GLUBBITY-GLUB!
SPLASH! SPLOOSH! SPLISH![3]

A big crowd gathered at the shore.
They cheered and clapped and
called for more!
Her friends cried out . . .

"Hurray!" "Encore!"
"Hilda, keep on dancing!"
And so . . . she did.

Think Aloud

[3]I notice the author changes the sounds to go along with Hilda's moves or the place where she is dancing. These are sounds you might hear when someone is moving around in water.

After Reading

Retell: Invite children to draw a picture to show a part of the story they enjoyed the most. Have them use their pictures to retell the story.

Student Think Aloud

Use Copying Master number 3 to prompt children to describe something that they visualized in the story.

"I was able to picture in my mind . . ."

Cultural Perspective

Flamenco dancing comes from Spain. It is a combination of guitar playing, singing, dancing, and handclapping.

Think and Respond

1. Why did the other animals enjoy Hilda's dance in the water? *Possible response: She didn't cause the jungle floor to shake because she was floating in the water.* **Inferential**

2. Name things that the animals do in this fantasy story that they can't do in real life. *Possible responses: dance, talk, knit, sing* **Genre**

3. Why do you think the author wrote this story? *Possible responses: She wanted to make us laugh; to show that we can express ourselves in different ways no matter who we are.* **Author's Purpose**

The Wheels on the Bus

a song
retold by Ann Owen

Genre: Traditional Song

Poetic Element: Rhythmic Patterns

Comprehension Strategy: Visualize

Think-Aloud Copying Master number 3

 Before Reading

Genre: Tell children that "The Wheels on the Bus" is actually a song that they might recognize. Explain that the words to the song are a poem with repeating words and a pattern. Invite children to recall another song that they have heard or sung, such as "The Hokey Pokey."

Expand Vocabulary: Discuss these words and phrases before you read the story:

> *wipers:* long rubber parts that clean a windshield
>
> *move on back:* walk to the back of the bus to sit down
>
> *yak yak yak:* a humorous way to describe talking

Set a Purpose for Reading: Tell children to picture themselves riding on a bus as they listen to the sounds in the song.

 **During Reading**

Use the Think Aloud during the first reading of the story. Notes about the genre and the cultural perspective may be used during subsequent readings.

The Wheels on the Bus

edited by Ann Owen

1. The wheels on the bus go round and round,
   Round and round, round and round.
   The wheels on the bus go round and round,
   All around the town.

2. The wipers on the bus go swish swish swish.
   Swish swish swish, swish swish swish.
   The wipers on the bus go swish swish swish,
   All around the town.

3. The driver on the bus goes "Move on back!
   Move on back, move on back!"
   The driver on the bus goes "Move on back!"
   All around the town.

4. The people on the bus go up and down.
   Up and down, up and down.
   The people on the bus go up and down.
   All around the town.

5. The horn on the bus goes beep beep beep.
   Beep beep beep, beep beep beep.
   The horn on the bus goes beep beep beep.
   All around the town.

6. The kids on the bus go "Yak yak yak.
   Yak yak yak, yak yak yak."
   The kids on the bus go "Yak yak yak."
   All around the town.

7. The baby on the bus goes "Wah wah wah,
   Wah wah wah, wah wah wah."
   The baby on the bus goes "Wah wah wah,"
   All around the town.

8. The parents on the bus go "Shh shh shh,
   Shh shh shh, shh shh shh."[1]
   The parents on the bus go "Shh shh shh,"
   All around the town.

9. The wheels on the bus go round and round,
   Round and round, round and round.
   The wheels on the bus go round and round,
   All around the town.

Think Aloud

[1] *I am able to picture in my mind the parents going "Shh shh shh!" I can see the kids on the bus being loud and bothering the people around them.*

Retell: Have the children sing the song, while pantomiming the actions described.

Student Think Aloud

Use Copying Master number 3 to prompt children to describe what they visualize when they sing or listen to this song.

"I was able to picture in my mind . . ."

Cultural Perspective

People travel on double-decker buses in England, Hong Kong, and Singapore. These buses are two-story, with stairs that lead to the second floor and its seats. They are twice as high as a regular bus.

Think and Respond

1. What is another sound you might hear on a bus? Make up another verse for the song. *Responses will vary. Possible response: The dogs on the bus go ruff, ruff, ruff.* **Critical**

2. How is this song like a poem? *Possible response: It has rhythm and a pattern.* **Genre**

3. Why do you think the author wrote this selection? *Possible response: to entertain us with a song about a silly situation that is fun to sing about* **Author's Purpose**

Turtle's Race with Beaver

a folk tale

retold by Joseph Bruchac and James Bruchac

Genre: Folk Tale

Comprehension Strategy: Visualize

Think-Aloud Copying Master number 1

Before Reading

Genre: Tell children that "Turtle's Race with Beaver" is a folk tale, a story that has been handed down for many years. Point out that folk tales often include animals that talk and act like people. Ask them to recall other folk tales they have listened to, such as "The Three Billy Goats Gruff."

Expand Vocabulary: Introduce these words and phrases before you begin reading:

> *sun:* warm up by sitting under the sun
>
> *dam:* a wall built across a stream to hold back the flow of water
>
> *lodge:* the name of a beaver's home
>
> *shallower:* not as deep as before

Set a Purpose for Reading: Have children listen to see who wins the race and what causes this to happen.

During Reading

Use the Think Alouds during the first reading of the story. Notes about the genre and the cultural perspective may be used during subsequent readings.

Turtle's Race with Beaver

as told by Joseph Bruchac and James Bruchac

Long ago, Turtle lived in a beautiful little pond.

She was very happy because this pond had everything a turtle needed. The water was just deep enough, there was plenty of food to eat, and there were lots of nice rocks just above the water for Turtle to sun herself on.

One day, as happens every year in the north, winter began to come to the land. As she had done year after year, Turtle swam to the bottom of the pond and buried herself in the thick mud.[1]

While Turtle slept for the winter, another animal came walking along. It was Beaver, who had been looking for a new home.

"This will be perfect," said Beaver, "once I make some changes."

Soon he began doing one of the things beavers do so well. Chomp! Chomp! went Beaver as he took down one tree after another to build a big dam.

He worked hard for many days. And as he did, the water got deeper and deeper.

After finishing the dam, Beaver made himself a fine lodge of mud and sticks, then settled in for the rest of the winter. He was very happy.

The moon came and went, and spring returned once more to the land. The birds sang and the ice melted away. Then Turtle woke up. Crawling out from under the mud, she began to swim toward the surface of the water. But she had to swim higher, and higher, and higher, and higher.

By the time Turtle made it to the surface, she realized that the water was four times as deep as before! Her pond didn't look the same at all. All of the rocks she loved to sun herself on were under water. On one side the pond stretched as far as the eyes could see. On the other stood a huge dam. Not too far from that was a big round lodge.

Then Turtle heard a loud *Whack!* She turned to see where the sound had come from. A strange animal was swimming toward her. It was Beaver.

"Who are you?" asked Beaver. "What are you doing here?"

"I am Turtle," Turtle said. "This is my pond. I have lived here my whole life."

Think Aloud

[1] *I was able to picture in my mind Turtle's little pond because the authors tell so much about it. I can imagine some nice smooth rocks for sunning, and plenty of bugs for Turtle to munch.*

"*Your* pond!" said Beaver. "This is *my* pond! Look at my wonderful dam and my splendid lodge. This is a beaver's pond."

"Yes," Turtle said, "I can see that you've done lots of work. Couldn't we just share the pond? There's plenty of room."

"Ha!" Beaver laughed. "I will not share my pond with any little turtle. But I *will* challenge you to a race. Whoever wins can stay, whoever loses must go find a new home."

Turtle didn't really want to race. She could see that Beaver, with his big flat tail, was probably a much faster swimmer. But this pond was the only home she knew.

"I agree," Turtle said. "We will race."[2]

It was decided that the race would take place the next morning at first light. The two would meet on one side of the pond and race to the other.

That night, Beaver told other animals about the race. Word began to spread throughout the forest.

Squirrel told Rabbit, Rabbit told Fox, Fox told Wolf, Wolf told Deer, Deer told Moose, Moose told Bear. Soon every animal in the forest knew.

Before first light came to the land, all of the animals of the forest gathered around the pond. As they waited for Turtle and Beaver to arrive, many chose sides. Most of the smaller animals, such as Chipmunk and Rabbit, sided with Turtle. Most of the bigger animals, such as Wolf, Moose, and Bear, sided with Beaver.

As they waited, they began to sing:

TURTLE! BEAVER! TURTLE!
BEAVER! TURTLE! BEAVER!

They sang even louder when Beaver came swimming over from his lodge and Turtle popped up from under the water.

TURTLE! BEAVER! TURTLE!
BEAVER! TURTLE! BEAVER!

Turtle and Beaver took their positions on the shore.

Bear lifted his big paw in the air. "On your mark . . . get set . . . GO!"

SPLASH! went Beaver, leaping off from the shore. He was certain he would leave Turtle far behind. But Turtle had gotten an idea. Before Beaver hit the water, Turtle stretched out her long neck, opened her mouth, and bit into the end of Beaver's tail.

FLAP! FLAP! FLAP! went Beaver, swimming as fast as he could. But as fast as he went, Turtle was right behind, holding on as hard as he could.

Think Aloud

[2] *I wonder why Turtle agrees to race Beaver when she knows he is faster than she is. Hmmm. I don't see how Turtle can win this race.*

Genre Study

Folk Tale: The words an author chooses in some folk tales can show how old the story is. In this tale, the author describes the rising of the sun as *first light*. This is more commonly known as dawn.

The other animals kept cheering, but now some of the bigger animals were cheering for Turtle instead of Beaver.

TURTLE! BEAVER! TURTLE!
BEAVER! TURTLE! *TURTLE!*

Soon Beaver was halfway across the pond. Even though Turtle was still holding on, it looked as if Beaver would win for sure. Then Turtle bit a little harder into Beaver's tail.

FLAP! FLAP! FLAP! Beaver swam even faster. Turtle still held on. Now more of the animals were cheering for Turtle.

TURTLE! BEAVER! TURTLE!
TURTLE! TURTLE! TURTLE![3]

Now they were almost to the other side. Beaver seemed sure to win. But Turtle bit as hard as she could into Beaver's tail. *CRUNCH!*

"YEEEE-OWWWW!" yelled Beaver. He flipped his big flat tail up and out of the water. When his tail reached its highest point, Turtle let go.

"Weeee!" sang Turtle as she flew through the air right over Beaver's head.

KA-THUNK! Turtle landed on the far shore and crawled across the finish line. Turtle had won the race. All the animals cheered.

TURTLE! TURTLE! TURTLE!
TURTLE! TURTLE! TURTLE!

Turtle was very pleased. But she could see how sad Beaver was. "I would still be happy to share my pond," she said.

But Beaver was so embarrassed that he left without another word.

Over time Beaver's dam fell apart and the water got shallower and shallower. Turtle had back all her wonderful rocks to sun herself on.

As for Beaver, he did find a new home in a pond not too far away. In that pond, though, there also lived a turtle.

"Can I share your pond with you?" Beaver asked.

"Of course," that other turtle said.

And so the two of them lived there happily through all the seasons to come.

Think Aloud

[3] *The author makes me feel like I am really watching this race. I can't wait to find out who is going to win!*

After Reading

Retell: Have children draw a picture to show a scene from the story. Have them use their pictures to retell the story.

Student Think Aloud

"I wonder . . ."

Use Copying Master number 1 to prompt children to share questions they had as they listened to the story.

Cultural Perspective

This story was originally a folk tale told by Native Americans from the Seneca Nation. The Seneca people still live in New York, Ohio, and in many other parts of the country.

Encourage children to recognize how various cultures are represented in different kinds of stories.

Think and Respond

1. Who do you think would make a better friend—Turtle or Beaver? Why? *Responses will vary. Possible response: Turtle would make a better friend because she is willing to share.* **Analytical**

2. How is this story like "The Tortoise and the Hare"? *Possible responses: No one expects Turtle or Tortoise to win the race because they are slow animals. However, they end up surprising everyone by winning their races.* **Genre**

3. Why do you think the author wrote this story? *Possible responses: to teach us that we should share with others; to warn us not to be too sure of ourselves.* **Author's Purpose**

Alexander Graham Bell

a biography
by Lola M. Schaefer

Genre: Biography

Comprehension Strategy: Generate Questions

Think-Aloud Copying Master number 4

 Before Reading

Genre: Ask children to recall the biography they recently heard about Johnny Appleseed. Remind them that a biography gives information about a real person. Tell them that this next story is a biography about a famous inventor, Alexander Graham Bell.

Expand Vocabulary: Before reading introduce these terms:

deaf: not able to hear

experiments: tests used to prove something

electricity: the power that lights lamps, provides heat, and makes appliances work

communicate: talk

Set a Purpose for Reading: Have children listen to find out what Alexander Graham Bell invented.

 **During Reading**

Use the Think Alouds during the first reading of the story. Notes about the genre and cultural perspective may be used during subsequent readings.

Alexander Graham Bell

by Lola M. Schaefer

Alexander Graham Bell was born in Scotland in 1847. His father was a famous teacher who taught people how to speak well.

Alexander's mother was deac. She was still able to teach him to play the piano. Alexander was good at music and science.[1]

Alexander was interested in sound. He also liked to invent things. He built a machine that could speak. He also tried to make his dog talk.

In 1871, Alexander moved to Boston. During the day, he taught deaf students how to speak. At night, he did experiments with sound.

Alexander wanted to learn more about electricity. In 1874, he met Tom Watson. Tom knew how electricity worked. They began to work together.

Alexander stopped teaching. He did experiments day and night. He and Tom wanted to invent a machine that could send voices from one place to another.

On March 10, 1876, Alexander and Tom reached their goal. Alexander spoke to Tom through the first telephone.[2]

Alexander and Tom made the telephone better. Soon it could send voices many miles. In 1915, they made the first telephone call across the United States.

Alexander spent his life inventing. He died in 1922. Alexander Graham Bell changed the way people communicate with one another.

Think Aloud

[1] *I wonder how Alexander's mother taught him to play the piano. She couldn't hear him practicing because she was deaf. She must have been a good teacher because the author says that Alexander was good at music.*

Think Aloud

[2] *I figured out that Bell and Watson made a great team because Bell knew about sound and Watson knew about electricity. They shared information with each other.*

After Reading

Retell: Have children list two facts that they learned about Alexander Graham Bell while listening to the selection. Have children discuss what inventors do. Then have them identify people they know about who have invented or discovered something.

Student Think Aloud

Use Copying Master number 4 to prompt children to share something they figured out while listening to this biography.

"I figured out _____ because . . ."

Cultural Perspective

The country of France awarded Bell about $10,000 for his invention of the telephone. He used the money to develop the Graphophone, which made recordings of sounds.

Think and Respond

1. What things did Alexander Graham Bell do to show he was interested in sound? *Possible response: he played piano; he built a talking machine; he tried to teach his dog to speak; he experimented with sound.* **Inferential**

2. Is this biography arranged in time order? How do you know? *Possible response: Yes, it is in time order, like a timeline, because there are years and dates listed and they go in order.* **Genre**

3. Why did Lola M. Schaefer write this story? *Possible response: She wanted to give readers information about Alexander Graham Bell.* **Author's Purpose**

THE SOUND OF MUSIC

by Ringo H. W. Chiu

Genre: Nonfiction
Comprehension Strategy: Generate Questions
Think-Aloud Copying Master number 5

Before Reading

Genre: Remind children that nonfiction selections give readers information about a topic. Invite children to recall other nonfiction stories they have heard, such as "The Power of Weather."

Expand Vocabulary: Introduce these words and phrases before you read the story:

> *performance:* a public show or entertainment
>
> *pays tribute:* honors
>
> *heritage:* something that is handed down from one's ancestors
>
> *stereo:* a sound system

Set a Purpose for Reading: Have children listen to this story to find out why a composer made musical instruments out of paper.

During Reading

Use the Think Alouds during the first reading of the story. Notes about the genre and the cultural perspective may be used during subsequent readings.

THE SOUND OF MUSIC

by Ringo H. W. Chiu

What shakes, pops, cracks, crumbles, tears, puckers, slaps, whistles, and sings? Give up? Those are just some of the many sounds that people can make with paper.[1]

PAPER INSTRUMENTS

In October 2003, fifth graders watched as rolls of paper were released from the ceiling at the new Walt Disney Concert Hall in Los Angeles. Waving the paper, tapping on it, or blowing on it were some of the many ways musicians made sounds.

The paper instruments were part of a special performance called *Inventions for Paper Instruments and Orchestra*. Chinese composer Tan Dun wrote the piece. He also invented and made the paper instruments used in the performance.

Dun's piece honors the art of papermaking and pays tribute to his Chinese heritage. Paper as we know it today was invented about 2,000 years ago in China.

BRINGING MUSIC TO LIFE

The paper instruments allowed schoolchildren to hear how the shape of the concert hall affects sound. One 10-year-old girl from Los Angeles said that the concert hall sounded "like a giant stereo."

Dun says that the performance shows children that music can come from everyday objects. "Using your imagination, you can find music around you, even in paper," Dun says. "Music is everywhere if you just look for it."[2]

After Reading

Retell: Have children list two facts that they learned while listening to the selection.

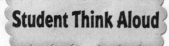

Use Copying Master number 5 to prompt children to tell about how the author wrote this story.

"I noticed the author . . ."

Cultural Perspective

The earliest paper from China was made from mixing mulberry tree bark and bamboo plant fiber with water. This mixture was pounded with a special tool and left to dry on a piece of cloth.

Think and Respond

1. What objects in your classroom could you use to make music? *Responses will vary.* **Analytical**

2. The first line of the story is a riddle or guessing game about sounds. Why do you think the story begins this way? *Possible response: It makes us want to guess the answer and listen to find out.* **Genre**

3. Why does the author think it is important to share this story with others? *Possible response: It gives information about interesting paper instruments and about the history of paper.* **Author's Purpose**

The Enormous Turnip

a folk tale
retold by Kathy Parkinson

Genre: Folk Tale

Comprehension Strategy: Generate Questions

Think-Aloud Copying Master number 3

Before Reading

Genre: Remind children that a folk tale is a story that has been told and retold for many, many years. Folk tales often have repeating sections that make the story fun to hear. Tell children that the story they will hear is about an enormous turnip. Ask children to tell about other folk tales they have heard, such as "The Gingerbread Man."

Expand Vocabulary: Introduce these words before reading:

> *turnip:* a vegetable that grows underground

> *heaved:* pulled

> *enormous:* huge

Set a Purpose for Reading: Ask children to listen to find out what happens when a man tries to pull up an enormous turnip.

During Reading

Use the Think Alouds during the first reading of the story. Notes about the genre and cultural perspective may be used during subsequent readings.

The Enormous Turnip

by Kathy Parkinson

There was once a man who had a vegetable garden that was his pride and joy. Every day he was out in his garden, digging and hoeing, weeding, and watering. One day he planted two rows of turnip seeds. In no time at all the first little leaves poked through the soil and soon the plants were growing strongly.

But one plant was growing more strongly than all the rest! It grew and it grew and it grew, until it was the biggest turnip that anyone had ever seen.

At last the day came when the man decided to go out into his garden to pull up his turnip. He grasped hold of the leaves, counted to three and HEAVED . . . but he could not pull up the enormous turnip.[1]

So the man called to his wife. "Please come and help me pull up this turnip!" he cried. His wife put her arms around his waist and the man counted to three and . . . HEAVED! But they could not pull up the enormous turnip.

A little boy was passing by. "Please come and help us pull up this turnip!" cried the man and his wife. The little boy put his arms around the woman's waist. The man counted to three and . . . HEAVED! But they could not pull up the enormous turnip.

The little boy saw his sister walking by. "Come and help us pull up this turnip!" he cried. The little girl put her arms around her brother's waist. The man counted to three and . . . HEAVED! But they could not pull up the enormous turnip.[2]

The little girl saw her dog by the fence. "Come and help us pull up this turnip!" she cried. The dog took hold of the little girl's skirt in his mouth. The man counted to three and . . . HEAVED! But they could not pull up the enormous turnip.

The dog saw a cat in a tree. "Come and help us pull up this turnip!" he barked. The cat took hold of the dog's tail. The man counted to three and . . . HEAVED! But they could not pull up the enormous turnip.

The cat spied a little mouse under a cabbage. "Come and help us pull up this turnip!" she meowed. The mouse took hold of the cat's tail in her mouth. The man counted to three and . . . HEAVED! The turnip flew out of the ground so fast that the man and the woman and the little boy and the little girl and the dog and the cat and the mouse all fell on top of each other![3]

Genre Study

Folk Tale: Since folk tales are passed on by storytellers, they often have repeating sections to make the story easier to remember. In this story, sentences are repeated each time a new character tries to help pull up the turnip.

Think Aloud

[1] *I wonder what the man will do to pull up that big turnip. I think he needs some help.*

Think Aloud

[2] *I was able to picture in my mind the strange sight of all these people pulling the turnip. It makes me wonder just how enormous this turnip really is!*

Think Aloud

[3] *I think it is funny that a little mouse is the character that actually makes a difference and helps get the turnip out of the ground.*

The man looked at the enormous turnip and scratched his head. He still had a problem.

"Please help me to eat this enormous turnip!" he cried. So the man and the woman and the little boy and the little girl and the dog and the cat and the mouse all sat down to supper together.

I wonder if they have finished yet?

After Reading

Retell the Story: Ask children to act out this story. Assign roles of the people and animals.

Student Think Aloud

Use Copying Master number 3 to prompt children to discuss something amusing they imagined from the story.

"I was able to picture in my mind . . ."

Cultural Perspective

This folk tale is from Russia, where the turnip is a common garden vegetable. Other versions of this story tell about a giant cabbage or potato.

Supply children with another version of the story, from a different place and time, and read it aloud. Encourage children to recognize the different cultural perspectives of the two stories. See the Unit 4 Theme Bibliography, page T24, for the suggested title: *The Turnip*.

Think and Respond

1. What was your favorite part of this story? Why? *Responses will vary. Possible response: I liked it when the dog asked the cat to help because dogs don't usually like cats.* **Critical**

2. How is this folk tale like "The Gingerbread Man"? *Possible response: They both have talking animals, repeating parts, make-believe things like giant turnips and a talking cookie.* **Genre**

3. What might the author want to teach you about the importance of working together? *Possible response: Hard things can be done when people help each other.* **Author's Purpose**

The Little Engine That Could

a story
retold by Watty Piper

Genre: Fiction

Comprehension Strategy: Generate Questions

Think-Aloud Copying Master number 1

 Before Reading

Genre: Tell children that a fiction story is made up by an author. Characters in a fiction story might be people, animals, or even toys and trains. Help children recall another fiction story they heard called "Make Way for Ducklings."

Expand Vocabulary: Before reading, introduce these terms:

> *jolly:* happy
>
> *berths:* beds
>
> *bellowed:* shouted
>
> *hitched:* connected

Set a Purpose for Reading: Have children read to find out what happens when a little train cannot get over the mountain.

 **During Reading**

Use the Think Alouds during the first reading of the story. The genre note may be used during subsequent readings.

The Little Engine That Could

retold by Watty Piper

Chug, chug, chug. Puff, puff, puff. Ding-dong, ding-dong. The little train rumbled over the tracks.

She was a happy little train for she had such a jolly load to carry. Her cars were full of good things for boys and girls.

There were toy animals—giraffes with long necks, Teddy bears with almost no necks at all, and even a baby elephant.

Then there were dolls—dolls with blue eyes and yellow curls, dolls with brown eyes and brown bobbed heads, and the funniest little toy clown you ever saw.

And there were cars full of toy engines, airplanes, tops, jack-knives, picture puzzles, books, and every kind of thing boys or girls could want.

But that was not all. Some of the cars were filled with all sorts of good things for boys and girls to eat—big golden oranges, red-cheeked apples, bottles of creamy milk for their breakfasts, fresh spinach for their dinners, peppermint drops, and lollypops for after-meal treats.

The little train was carrying all these wonderful things to the good little boys and girls on the other side of the mountain.

She puffed along merrily. Then all of a sudden she stopped with a jerk. She simply could not go another inch. She tried and she tried, but her wheels would not turn.

What were all those good little boys and girls on the other side of the mountain going to do without the wonderful toys to play with and the good food to eat?

"Here comes a shiny new engine," said the funny little clown who jumped out of the train.

"Let us ask him to help us."

So all the dolls and toys cried out together, "Please, Shiny New Engine, won't you please pull our train over the mountain? Our engine has broken down, and the boys and girls on the other side won't have any toys to play with or good food to eat unless you help us."[1]

But the Shiny New Engine snorted, "Pull you? I am a Passenger Engine. I have just carried a fine train over the mountain, with more cars than you ever dreamed of. My train had sleeping cars, with comfortable berths; a dining car where waiters bring whatever hungry people want to eat; and parlor cars

Genre Study

Fiction: Fiction stories often contain colorful details that describe the characters and setting. The details appeal to the readers' five senses and helps them picture what is happening in their minds.

Think Aloud

[1] *I know that dolls and toys can't talk in real life. This is a make-believe story.*

in which people sit in soft armchairs and look out of big plate-glass windows. I pull the likes of you? Indeed not!"

And off he steamed to the roundhouse, where engines live when they are not busy. How sad the little train and all the dolls and toys felt!

Then the little clown called out, "The Passenger Engine is not the only one in the world. Here is another engine coming, a great big strong one. Let us ask him to help us."

The little toy clown waved his flag and the big strong engine came to a stop.

"Please, oh, please, Big Engine," cried all the dolls and toys together. "Won't you please pull our train over the mountain? Our engine has broken down, and the good little boys and girls on the other side won't have any toys to play with or good food to eat unless you help us."

But the Big Strong Engine <u>bellowed</u>, "I am a Freight Engine. I have just pulled a big train loaded with big machines over the mountain. These machines print books and newspapers for grown-ups to read. I am a very important engine indeed. I won't pull the likes of you!" And the Freight Engine puffed off indignantly to the roundhouse.[2]

The little train and all the dolls and toys were very sad.

"Cheer up," cried the little toy clown. "The Freight Engine is not the only one in the world. Here comes another. He looks very old and tired, but our train is so little, perhaps he can help us."

So the little toy clown waved his flag and the dingy, rusty old engine stopped.

"Please, Kind Engine," cried all the dolls and toys together. "Won't you please pull our train over the mountain? Our engine has broken down, and the boys and girls on the other side won't have any toys to play with or good food to eat unless you help us."

But the Rusty Old Engine sighed, "I am so tired. I must rest my weary wheels. I cannot pull even so little a train as yours over the mountain. I can not. I can not. I can not."

And off he rumbled to the roundhouse chugging, "I can not. I can not. I can not."

Then indeed the little train was very, very sad, and the dolls and toys were ready to cry.

But the little clown called out, "Here is another engine coming, a little blue engine, a very little one. Maybe she will help us."

Think Aloud

[2] *I wonder who will stop and help the little train. At first I thought the Big Strong Engine would help but then I found out that this train is not very nice at all.*

The very little engine came chug, chugging merrily along. When she saw the toy clown's flag, she stopped quickly.

"What is the matter, my friends?" she asked kindly.

"Oh, Little Blue Engine," cried the dolls and toys. "Will you pull us over the mountain? Our engine has broken down and the good boys and girls on the other side won't have any toys to play with or good food to eat, unless you help us. Please, please help us, Little Blue Engine."

"I'm not very big," said the Little Blue Engine. "They use me only for switching trains in the yard. I have never been over the mountain."

"But we must get over the mountain before the children awake," said all the dolls and the toys.

The very little engine looked up and saw the tears in the dolls' eyes. And she thought of the good little boys and girls on the other side of the mountain who would not have any toys or good food unless she helped.

Then she said, "I think I can. I think I can. I think I can." And she hitched herself to the little train.[3]

She tugged and pulled and pulled and tugged and slowly, slowly, slowly they started off.

The toy clown jumped aboard and all the dolls and the toy animals began to smile and cheer.

Puff, puff, chug, chug, went the Little Blue Engine. "I think I can—I think I can—I think I can—I think I can—I think I can—I think I can—I think I can—I think I can—I think I can."

Up, up, up. Faster and faster and faster the little engine climbed, until at last they reached the top of the mountain.

Down in the valley lay the city.

"Hurray, hurray," cried the funny little clown and all the dolls and toys. "The good little boys and girls in the city will be happy because you helped us, kind Little Blue Engine."

And the Little Blue Engine smiled and seemed to say as she puffed steadily down the mountain . . .

"I thought I could. I thought I could. I thought I could.
    I thought I could.
        I thought I could.
            I thought I could."

Think Aloud

[3] The little blue engine sounds like she is trying very hard to pull the train. I think that she is going to make it over the mountain. I will listen to find out.

After Reading

Retell: Have children act out the story. Assign roles of the trains and toys.

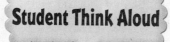

Student Think Aloud

Use Copying Master number 1 to prompt children to share something that they had a question about while listening to the story.

"I wonder . . ."

Think and Respond

1. What words would you use to describe the little blue engine? *Possible responses: brave, kind, hard-working, helpful* **Critical**

2. How is this fiction story different from a biography like "Alexander Graham Bell"? *Possible responses: This story is make-believe and does not contain facts about a real person.* **Genre**

3. Why do you think the author repeats the words "I think I can" so many times? *Possible responses: When you read them aloud they sound like the rhythm of a moving train. He wants to emphasize the importance of believing in yourself.* **Author's Purpose**

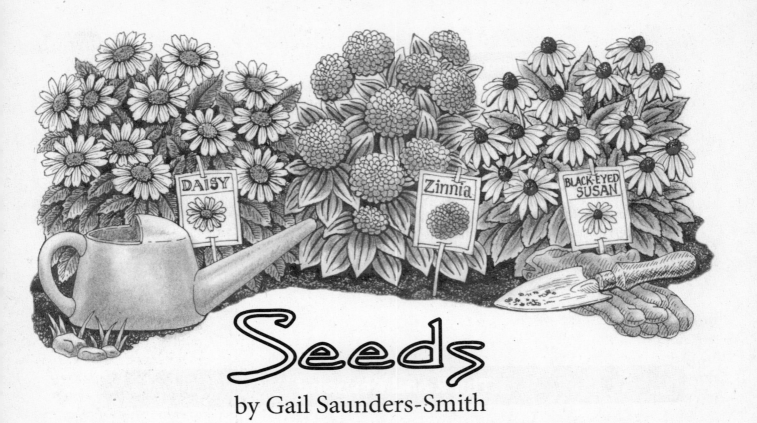

Seeds

by Gail Saunders-Smith

Genre: Nonfiction

Comprehension Strategy: Generate Questions

Think-Aloud Copying Master number 1

 Before Reading

Genre: Explain that "Seeds" is a nonfiction story. Remind children that nonfiction tells facts about a topic. Then have them recall other nonfiction stories they have heard, such as "The Sound of Music" and "Tooth Tales from Around the World."

Expand Vocabulary: Introduce these words before reading the story:

soil: dirt

roots: the parts of the plant that grow under the ground

stem: the part of the plant that the leaves grow from

Set a Purpose for Reading: Ask children to listen to find out what causes seeds to grow.

 **During Reading**

Use the Think Alouds during the first reading of the story. The genre note may be used during subsequent readings.

Seeds

by Gail Saunders-Smith

A flower is the part of a plant that makes seeds. Seeds form after the flower blooms. New plants can grow from seeds.

Flower seeds are different sizes, shapes, and colors. Some seeds are long, and some are short. Some seeds are small, and some are big.[1] Each kind of seed grows into a different kind of flower.

People plant flower seeds. They place the flower seeds in holes in the ground. People cover the seeds with <u>soil</u>. Then they water the seeds.

Nature also plants flower seeds. Some seeds fall from the old flower. These seeds go into the soil. New plants grow near the old plants.[2]

Birds eat flower seeds. They scatter some seeds on the ground. They drop some seeds in places far away.

The wind moves seeds. Some seeds have soft hairs. These hairs catch the wind. The seeds float to new places where they can grow.[3]

Seeds need air, water, and warmth to grow. They also need food found in the soil.

A seed takes in water. Then it breaks open. A new plant is inside the seed.

The new plant grows <u>roots</u>. Roots grow down. The new plant grows a <u>stem</u>. The stem grows up through the soil. The stem grows into a flower.

 **After Reading**

Retell: Have children list three facts they learned about seeds while listening to the selection.

 **Student Think Aloud**

Use Copying Master number 1 to prompt children to share questions they had about the selection.

"I wonder . . ."

Think and Respond

1. Why are seeds different sizes and shapes? *Possible responses: They grow into different plants and flowers; some plants are big and some are little.* **Inferential**

2. How can you tell this story is nonfiction? *Possible responses: it gives facts and information about something. It is not make-believe.* **Genre**

3. Why do you think authors write selections like "Seeds"? *Possible response: to teach facts about nature.* **Author's Purpose**

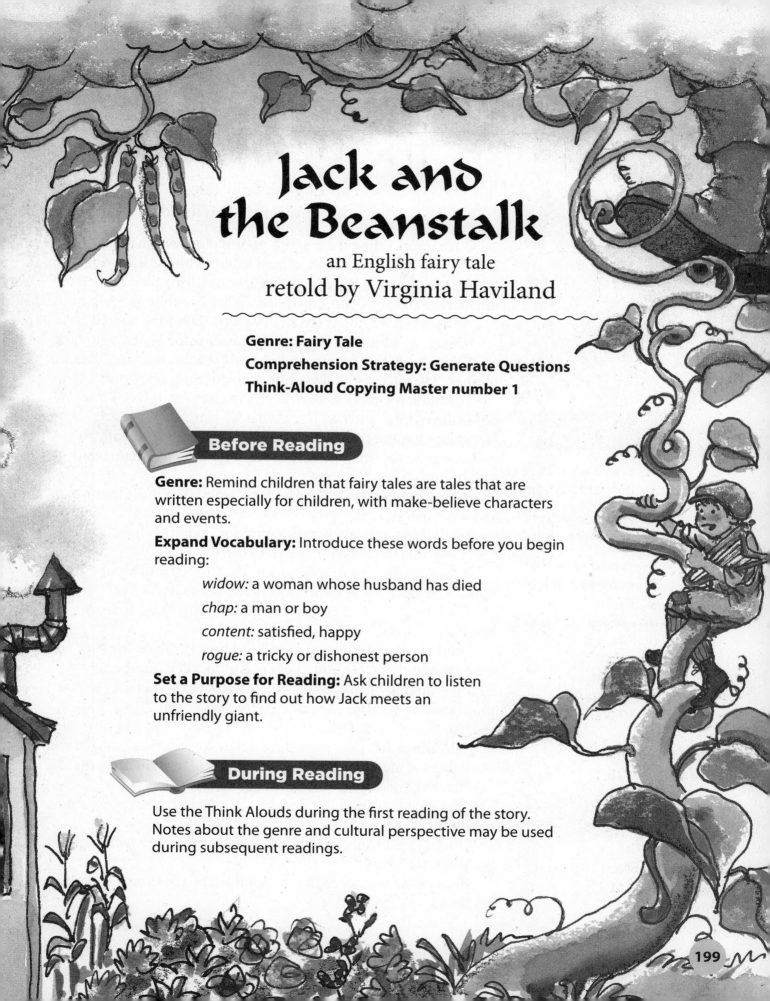

Jack and the Beanstalk

an English fairy tale
retold by Virginia Haviland

Genre: Fairy Tale

Comprehension Strategy: Generate Questions

Think-Aloud Copying Master number 1

Before Reading

Genre: Remind children that fairy tales are tales that are written especially for children, with make-believe characters and events.

Expand Vocabulary: Introduce these words before you begin reading:

widow: a woman whose husband has died

chap: a man or boy

content: satisfied, happy

rogue: a tricky or dishonest person

Set a Purpose for Reading: Ask children to listen to the story to find out how Jack meets an unfriendly giant.

During Reading

Use the Think Alouds during the first reading of the story. Notes about the genre and cultural perspective may be used during subsequent readings.

Jack and the Beanstalk

an English fairy tale
retold by Virginia Haviland

Once upon a time there was a poor <u>widow</u> who had an only son, named Jack, and a cow, named Milky-white. All they had to live on was the milk the cow gave every day. This they carried to the market and sold. But one morning Milky-white gave no milk.

"What shall we do? What shall we do?" cried the widow.

"Cheer up, Mother! I'll go and get work somewhere," said Jack.

"We've tried that before, and nobody would take you," said his mother. "We must sell Milky-white and with the money start a shop."

"All right, Mother," said Jack. "It's market day today. I'll soon sell Milky-white. Then we'll see what we can do."

So he took the cow's halter in his hand, and started off. He had not gone far when he met a funny-looking old man, who said to him, "Good morning, Jack."

"Good morning to you," said Jack, wondering how the man knew his name.

"Well, Jack, and where are you off to?" said the man.

"I'm going to market to sell our cow."

"Oh, you look the proper sort of <u>chap</u> to sell cows," said the man. "I wonder if you know how many beans make five."

"Two in each hand and one in your mouth," said Jack, as sharp as a needle.[1]

"Right you are," said the man, "and here they are, the very beans themselves." He pulled out of his pocket a number of strange-looking beans. "Since you are so sharp," said he, "I don't mind trading with you—your cow for these beans."

"Go along!" said Jack.

"Ah! You don't know what these beans are," said the man. "If you plant them at night, by morning the stalks will be right up to the sky."

"Really?" said Jack. "You don't say so."

"Yes, that is so, and if it doesn't turn out to be true, you can have your cow back."

"Right," said Jack. He handed over Milky-white's halter and pocketed the beans.[2]

Back home went Jack. It was not dusk by the time he got to his door.

Think Aloud

[1] I wonder what "sharp as a needle" means. The man asks Jack a question that sounds tricky, and Jack answers him. So I think the word *sharp* in this case means "smart."

Think Aloud

[2] Uh oh! I don't think Jack's mother is going to be happy when Jack brings beans home instead of money!

"Back already, Jack?" said his mother. "I see you haven't got Milky-white, so you've sold her. How much did you get for her?"

"You'll never guess, Mother," said Jack.

"No, you don't say so! Good boy! Five pounds? Ten? Fifteen? No, it can't be twenty!"

"I told you you couldn't guess. What do you say to these beans? They're magical—plant them at night and . . .

"What!" said Jack's mother. "Have you been such a fool as to give away my Milky-white for a set of dry beans? Take that! Take that! Take that!" and she gave him three hard slaps. "As for your magic beans, here they go out of the window. Now off with you to bed. Not a drop shall you drink and not a bite shall you swallow this very night."

So Jack went upstairs to his little room in the attic. Sad and sorry he was, to be sure.

At last he dropped off to sleep.

When he woke up, his room looked very strange! The sun was shining, yet the room seemed dark and shadowy. Jack jumped up and ran to the window. What do you think he saw? Why, the beans his mother had thrown out of the window into the garden had sprung up into a big beanstalk. It went up and up and up till it reached the sky. The old man had spoken the truth after all.

The beanstalk grew close to Jack's window and ran up beyond like a great ladder. So Jack jumped onto the beanstalk, and began to climb. He climbed, and he climbed, and he climbed, and he climbed, and he climbed, and he climbed, and he climbed. At last, through the clouds, he reached the sky. When he got there he found a long, broad road going on as straight as an arrow. So he walked along, and he walked along, and he walked along till he came to a great tall house. On the doorstep there was a great tall woman.

"Good morning, mum," said Jack, quite polite. "Could you be so kind as to give me some breakfast?" For he hadn't had anything to eat the night before, you know. He was as hungry as a hunter.

"It's breakfast you want, is it?" said the great tall woman. "It's breakfast you'll be if you don't move off from here. My man is a giant, and there's nothing he likes better than boys broiled on toast. You'd better be moving on or he'll soon be coming."

"Oh! Please, mum, do give me something to eat, mum. I've had nothing since yesterday morning, really and truly, mum," said Jack. "I may as well be broiled as die of hunger."

Well, the giant's wife was not half so bad after all. She took Jack into the kitchen, and gave him a chunk of bread and cheese and jug of milk. But Jack hadn't half finished these when— *thump! thump! thump!*—the whole house began to tremble with the noise of someone coming.

"Goodness gracious me! It's my old man," said the giant's wife. "What on earth shall I do? Come along quick and jump in here." She bundled Jack into the oven, just as the giant came in.

He was a big man, to be sure. At his belt he had three calves strung up by the heels. He threw them down on the table and said, "Here, wife, broil me two of these for breakfast. Ah! What's this I smell?. . .

"Fee-fi-fo-fum.
I smell the blood of an Englishman!
Be he alive, or be he dead,
I'll grind his bones to make my bread."

"Nonsense, dear," said his wife. "You're dreaming. Or perhaps you smell the scraps of that little boy you liked so much for yesterday's dinner. Here, go wash and tidy up. By the time you come back your breakfast will be ready for you."

Off the giant went. Jack was just going to jump out of the oven and run away when the woman told him not to. "Wait till he's asleep," said she. "He always has a nap after breakfast."

The giant had his breakfast. After that he went to a big chest and took out of it two bags of gold. Down he sat and counted till at last his head began to nod. He began to snore till the whole house shook again.

Then Jack crept out on tiptoe from his oven. As he passed the giant, he took one of the bags of gold under his arm. Off he ran till he came to the beanstalk. He threw down the bag of gold, which of course fell into his mother's garden. He climbed down and climbed down till at last he got home. He told his mother what had happened and showed her the gold.

"Well, Mother," he said, "wasn't I right about the beans? They *are* really magical, you see."

They lived on the bag of gold for some time, but at last they came to the end of it. Jack made up his mind to try his luck once more at the top of the beanstalk. So one fine morning he rose early and got onto the beanstalk. He climbed, and he climbed, and he climbed, and he climbed, and he climbed, and he climbed, and he climbed. At last he

Genre Study

Fairy Tale: Authors often exaggerate features or powers of fairy tale characters. They make them seem larger than life. In this story, the giant is so big he can have three calves, or baby cows, hanging from his belt.

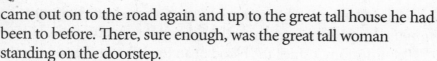

came out on to the road again and up to the great tall house he had been to before. There, sure enough, was the great tall woman standing on the doorstep.

"Good morning, mum," said Jack, as bold as brass. "Could you be so good as to give me something to eat?"

"Go away, my boy," said the great tall woman, "or else my man will eat you up for breakfast. But aren't you the boy who came here once before? Do you know, that very day my man missed one of his bags of gold!"

"That's strange, mum," said Jack. "I dare say I could tell you something about that. But I'm so hungry I can't speak till I've had something to eat."

Well, the great tall woman was so curious that she took him in and gave him something to eat. But he had scarcely begun munching it, as slowly as he could, when—*thump! thump! thump!*—they heard the giant's footstep, and his wife again hid Jack in the oven.

Everything happened as it did before. In came the giant, roaring "Fee-fi-fo-fum," and had his breakfast of three broiled oxen. Then he ordered, "Wife, bring me the hen that lays the golden eggs."

So she brought it. Her husband said, "Lay," and the hen laid an egg all of gold. But then the giant began to nod his head and to snore till the house shook.

Now Jack crept out of the oven on tiptoe and caught hold of the golden hen. He was off before you could say "Jack Robinson." This time, the giant woke—because the hen gave a cackle. Just as Jack got out of the house, he heard the giant calling, "Wife, wife, what have you done with my golden hen?"

And the wife said, "Why, my dear?"

But that was all Jack heard, for he rushed off to the beanstalk and climbed down in a flash. When he got home he showed his mother the wonderful hen, and said, "Lay!" to it. It laid a golden egg every time he said, "Lay!"

Well, Jack was not <u>content</u>. It wasn't very long before he decided to try his luck again up there at the top of the beanstalk. One fine morning he rose early and stepped onto the beanstalk. He climbed, and he climbed, and he climbed, and he climbed, till he came to the very top. This time he knew better than to go straight to the giant's house. When he came near it, he waited behind a bush till he saw the giant's wife come out with a pail to get some water. Then he crept into the house and hid in a

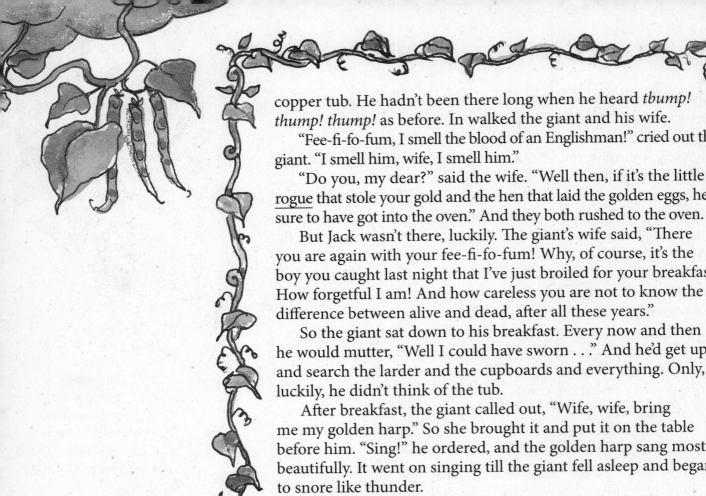

copper tub. He hadn't been there long when he heard *thump! thump! thump!* as before. In walked the giant and his wife.

"Fee-fi-fo-fum, I smell the blood of an Englishman!" cried out the giant. "I smell him, wife, I smell him."

"Do you, my dear?" said the wife. "Well then, if it's the little rogue that stole your gold and the hen that laid the golden eggs, he's sure to have got into the oven." And they both rushed to the oven.

But Jack wasn't there, luckily. The giant's wife said, "There you are again with your fee-fi-fo-fum! Why, of course, it's the boy you caught last night that I've just broiled for your breakfast. How forgetful I am! And how careless you are not to know the difference between alive and dead, after all these years."

So the giant sat down to his breakfast. Every now and then he would mutter, "Well I could have sworn . . ." And he'd get up and search the larder and the cupboards and everything. Only, luckily, he didn't think of the tub.

After breakfast, the giant called out, "Wife, wife, bring me my golden harp." So she brought it and put it on the table before him. "Sing!" he ordered, and the golden harp sang most beautifully. It went on singing till the giant fell asleep and began to snore like thunder.

Jack now got out of the tub very quietly and crept like a mouse over to the table. Up he crawled, caught hold of the golden harp, and dashed with it toward the door. But the harp called out quite loudly, "Master! Master!"

The giant woke up just in time to see Jack running off with his harp.

Jack ran as fast as he could. The giant came rushing after, and would soon have caught him, only Jack had a head start and knew where he was going. When he got to the beanstalk, the giant was not more than twenty yards away. Suddenly Jack disappeared. When the giant came to the end of the road, he saw Jack below climbing down for dear life.

Well, the giant didn't like to trust himself to such a ladder. He stood and waited, so Jack got another start.

But the harp cried out again, "Master! Master!"

The giant swung himself down onto the beanstalk, which shook with his weight. Down climbed Jack, and after him climbed the giant.

Jack climbed down, and climbed down, and climbed down till he was very nearly home. Then he called out, "Mother!

Mother! Bring me an ax, bring me an ax!" His mother rushed out with the ax in her hand. When she came to the beanstalk, she stood stock-still with fright. There was the giant with his legs just through the clouds.

Jack jumped down, took the ax, and chopped at the beanstalk, almost cutting it in two. The giant felt the beanstalk shake, so he stopped to see what the matter was. Then Jack chopped again. The beanstalk was cut in two. It began to topple over.[3] Down crashed the giant, and that was the end of him!

Jack gave his mother the golden harp. With the magical harp and the golden eggs, Jack and his mother became very rich. Jack married a Princess, and they all lived happily ever after.

Think Aloud

[3] *At first I think the giant will catch up to Jack on the beanstalk, and then I find out that Jack is able to chop the beanstalk down with the giant on it. Thank goodness! If Jack hadn't cut down that beanstalk, I'm afraid he would try to climb up it again!*

Retell the Story: Have children fold a sheet of drawing paper in half. On one side, have them draw a picture of something that happens to Jack before he climbs the beanstalk. On the other side, have them draw a picture of something that happens to Jack after he climbs the beanstalk.

Compare Different Versions: Explain to children that many versions of fairy tales exist from many places and time periods. Read a modern version of this tale from a different culture and era, and have children compare the characters, language, and other features of the tale. See unit 4 Theme Bibliography for the suggested title, *Jack and the Beanstalk*.

Student Think Aloud

"I wonder . . ."

Use Copying Master number 1 to prompt children to share a question they had about the story.

Cultural Perspective

The original author of this story is from England. In England, the word *pounds* does not refer to how much something weighs. Instead, *pounds* refers to a form of money used in England. Discuss with children the influence of the cultural and historical aspects of the fairy tale.

Think and Respond

1. Would you have climbed that beanstalk the third time if you were Jack? Why or why not? *Responses will vary. Possible response: No, I would not because I would not want to risk being eaten by the giant.* **Critical**

2. Why do children enjoy hearing fairy tales? *Responses will vary. Possible responses: Fairy tales help children use their imagination. Children enjoy listening to stories with magical things and characters in them.* **Genre**

3. This story has been around for a long time. Why do you think authors tell it over and over again? *Possible responses: It entertains people. It is fun imagining a beanstalk growing overnight and a giant at the top.* **Author's Purpose**

Hey, Bug!

a poem
by Lilian Moore

Genre: Poetry

Poetic Element: Rhyming Words and Humor

Comprehension Strategy: Draw Inferences

Think-Aloud Copying Master number 4

Before Reading

Genre: Tell children that the poem you will read aloud includes words that rhyme. Humorous poems, such as this one, often have rhyming words to make it fun to read. Remind children of other rhyming poems they have heard, such as "Growing Old" and "My Shadow."

Expand Vocabulary: Introduce these words before you begin reading the poem:

finger-hill: a finger stretched out to form a small hill

oatmeal: ground oats used to make cookies or cereal

crumb: a tiny piece of food

Set a Purpose for Reading: For the first reading, have children listen for rhyming words. Tell them to listen attentively so that they can tell the difference between a poem, a play, and a story.

During Reading

Read through the poem the first time without interruptions, emphasizing the rhyming words. Then reread and draw children's attention to the Think Aloud and genre note.

Think Aloud

[1]*I figured out that the bug doesn't really want to play with the speaker in this poem because the speaker is begging the bug not to go away!*

Hey, Bug!

by Lilian Moore

Hey, bug, stay!

Don't run away.

I know a game that we can play.

I'll hold my fingers very still

and you can climb a finger-hill.

No, no.

Don't go.[1]

Here's a wall—a tower, too,

a tiny bug town, just for you.

I've a cookie. You have some.

Take this oatmeal cookie crumb.

Hey, bug, stay!

Hey, bug!

Hey!

 **After Reading**

Retell: Have children draw a picture to show something described in the poem. Have them use rhyming words to tell about their pictures.

Student Think Aloud

Use Copying Master number 4 to prompt children to share something they figured out about the characters or action in this poem.

"I figured out _____ because . . ."

Think and Respond

1. How do you think the speaker feels about bugs? Why? *Possible response: the speaker probably likes bugs because he wants to play with one and share his food with it.* **Inferential**

2. Name some pairs of rhyming words in this poem. *Possible responses: stay/away/play; still/hill; no/go; too/you; some/crumb; stay/hey* **Genre**

3. How does this poem make you feel? Why do you think the poet wrote it? *Possible response: It makes me laugh because someone is talking to a bug! I think the poet wrote this poem to make people happy.* **Author's Purpose**

The Ant and the Pigeon

a fable from Africa
retold by Susan Kantor

Genre: Fable

Comprehension Strategy: Story Structure

Think-Aloud Copying Master number 6

Before Reading

Genre: Remind children that a fable is a story that teaches a lesson, or moral. Fables often have animal characters that act like people. Ask children to recall other fables they have listened to.

Expand Vocabulary: Before reading, introduce these terms:

> *exhausted:* worn out, very tired
>
> *pigeon:* a bird
>
> *desperately:* wildly, almost without hope

Set a Purpose for Reading: Ask children to listen to this story to find out how the pigeon and the ant help each other.

During Reading

Use the Think Alouds during the first reading of the story. Notes about the genre and cultural perspective may be used during subsequent readings.

The Ant and the Pigeon

a fable from Africa

An ant is saved by a pigeon, and almost immediately returns the favor.[1]

One day an ant found a grain of corn and decided to take it home. He held it very tight, and hurried as fast as he could, so that nothing would take the grain of corn from him. There was a pond on the way home, but the ant, in its haste, had forgotten about it, and he fell in, corn and all.

The corn slipped from his mouth and went to the bottom of the pond. The ant stayed on top of the water and worked hard to find a place to get out. But after a while, the ant began to be afraid that his strength was about <u>exhausted</u>.

A <u>pigeon</u> came to the pond to drink, and she saw the ant struggling <u>desperately</u>. She decided that she would help the little fellow. She took a long, dry piece of grass and dropped it so that it fell near the ant. He climbed on to the grass and soon got out.[2] The ant caught his breath, and then thanked the pigeon for saving him.

There was a boy near the pond with a bow and arrow. The ant saw him creeping up nearer and nearer to the pigeon. Hurrying as fast as he could, the ant climbed up the boy's leg and gave him a hard bite. The boy dropped his bow and arrow and cried out, and the pigeon saw him and flew to safety.

Each had saved the other. When the pigeon saved the ant she did not know that the ant would ever be able to do anything for her in return. Each was happier because of what each did for the other.[3]

The Bura people say, "Every person is another's butter." Even a small person can do something for a great person.

Think Aloud

[1]*With this sentence, the author tells me what the story is going to be about. It makes me curious about how a tiny little ant can help a bird like a pigeon.*

Think Aloud

[2]*I am able to picture in my mind just how the pigeon saves the ant. It is like throwing a rope to someone who is drowning.*

Think Aloud

[3]*I think this part of the story is important because it tells me the fable's lesson: to always be kind to others and to return good deeds. This story shows how kindness causes two friends to help each other.*

Retell the Story: Have children make paper-bag puppets of the ant and the pigeon and use them to reenact the events of the story.

Student Think Aloud

Use Copying Master number 6 to prompt children to share something they found important in the story.

"I thought _____ was important in this story because . . ."

Cultural Perspective

The Bura people live in Nigeria, a country in Africa. An African ant that lives there is known as the Bura ant because it is strong and fierce, like the Bura people.

Think and Respond

1. Do you believe that a small person can do something for a big person? Why or why not? *Responses will vary. Possible response: Yes, because a small person is just as important as a big one.* **Critical**

2. How is this fable like the fable "Anansi Saves Antelope"? *Possible responses: Two unlikely animals help each other. A small animal helps a big one. It teaches the same lesson.* **Genre**

3. What does the author want to teach you about the importance of returning favors? What does she want to show you about the importance of a person's size? *Possible response: She wants to teach me that people should return favors. She wants to show me that the size of a person doesn't matter.* **Author's Purpose**

One Giant Leap: The Story of Neil Armstrong

a biography
by Don Brown

Genre: Biography

Comprehension Strategy: Summarize

Think-Aloud Copying Master number 7

Before Reading

Genre: Remind children that a biography is a nonfiction story that is written about a real person by someone else to give information. Ask children to recall "Alexander Graham Bell," another biography they have listened to.

Expand Vocabulary: Introduce these words before you read the story:

propellers: blades that spin on the front of an airplane that help make it move

spectacle: an unusual sight

hovered: hung in the air

dough-mixing vats: large containers used to mix bread dough

Set a Purpose for Reading: Tell children that Neil Armstrong had a dream about doing something when he grew up. Have them listen to find out what that dream was.

During Reading

Use the Think Alouds during the first reading of the story. Notes about the genre and cultural perspective may be used during subsequent readings.

One Giant Leap: The Story of Neil Armstrong

by Don Brown

In 1932, two-year-old Neil Armstrong watched airplanes race.

Small, brightly colored planes flashed over Neil and his father, Stephen. The planes raced around a triangle-shaped course, their propellers tearing the sky with a sound that was like an endless thunderclap.

The spectacle surely left its mark on young Neil. Four years later, he leaped at the chance to ride in an airplane.

It wasn't on a racing plane but a three-motored passenger plane nicknamed the Tin Goose. The plane offered rides at the town airport. It could carry about a dozen people.

Neil and his father climbed aboard and buckled themselves into wicker seats. The engines sputtered to life with a terrific noise. The airplane raced down the runway and slowly lifted into the sky.

As the ground dropped farther and farther below them, people, houses, cars, *everything* looked smaller. The Tin Goose plowed through the clouds as gusts of wind bounced it up and down.

The noisy, bumpy ride and ever-tilting view worried Stephen Armstrong.

But Neil was fearless.

Neil was delighted.

Neil started making ten-cent airplane models and reading flying magazines.

He also started having a magical dream. In it, he held his breath and hovered above the ground. Below him, people, houses, cars, *everything* looked smaller.

As Neil grew, so did his interest in flying. Hundreds of model airplanes and stacks of *Air Travel* magazine began to appear in his bedroom.

A job mowing the Mission Cemetery lawn helped pay for it all.

At about the age of eleven, Neil worked for Neumeister's Bakery. Because he was small, Neil was placed into the dough-mixing vats to clean them.

He dreamed again and again of hovering.

When Neil was thirteen, the Armstrongs moved into a big white house on Benton Street in Wapakoneta, Ohio. Neil had been born in the living room of his grandparents' nearby farm on August 5, 1930.

Neil was shy and made friends carefully. Still, his life was busy. There was school and Boy Scouts. He played baritone horn in the school band and in a group called the Mississippi Moonshiners.

He flew rubber-band powered airplanes from a grassy hill.

He worked at the West End Market and Bowsher's Hardware, and he swept up and stocked shelves at Rhine and Brading's Pharmacy on Main Street.

On clear nights, Neil climbed to the roof of his neighbor Jacob Zint's garage. Mr. Zint had a homemade telescope mounted there and welcomed visitors to spy the moon and stars.

Neil looked and looked and looked.

A few miles from the Armstrongs' home, down the old brewery road, was the Port Koneta airport. Neil went there to watch the planes take off and land. Sometimes people paid him to wash their planes.

But watching and washing was not enough. Neil asked his parents if he could learn to fly. The lessons cost nine dollars an hour. He would have to work twenty-five hours to earn enough for one hour of flying.[1]

His parents agreed.

Soon afterward, Neil squeezed himself into a tiny Aeronca Champion airplane with his teacher, Aubrey Knudegard.

He learned to take off and land.

He learned to climb and swoop and bank.

He learned to follow a figure-eight path in the sky.

He learned that a pilot and an airplane together could be more than the person or the machine was alone.

Neil Armstrong earned his student pilot's license on his sixteenth birthday. He was too young to have an automobile driver's license.

In time, Neil Armstrong, student pilot, became Neil Armstrong, navy fighter pilot in the Korean War. Then he was Neil Armstrong, test pilot, flying rocket-powered airplanes to the upper edges of the sky. Eventually he became Neil Armstrong, astronaut.

Think Aloud

[1]*This is mostly about how hard Neil Armstrong is willing to work in order to pay for flying lessons.*

Astronauts are special pilots who fly spacecraft around Earth. When Neil became an astronaut there was a plan to land people on the moon and then return them safely to Earth. The moon had gripped people's imagination for thousands of years.

On July 16, 1969, astronauts Neil Armstrong, Buzz Aldrin, and Mike Collins sat in a cramped capsule atop a Saturn rocket. The Saturn was as big as an office building and powerful enough to fling three people more than 200,000 miles to the moon!

At 9:32 A.M. the main rocket motors erupted. Flames spewed from the Saturn's tail as it lifted from the ground. Soon the first set of engines exhausted their fuel and fell toward the ocean. Smaller engines sprang to life and sent the capsule circling the globe. After two turns around Earth, a final rocket engine blasted the capsule to 25,000 miles an hour and they hurtled to the moon.

Neil, Buzz, and Mike sped through black space for four days. The sun's light was broiling hot. The shadows were brutally cold. To prevent one side of the capsule from becoming overheated or frozen, it was turned slowly, like a hot dog on a grill. The astronauts called it the "barbecue roll."

When they reached the moon, Neil and Buzz entered a special spacecraft designed to part from the main capsule and land on the moon. Mike remained aboard the main capsule to pilot it as the other two astronauts dropped to the moon's surface.

A computer guided Neil and Buzz. But as they neared landing, Neil saw that there were large boulders in their way. He took control of the craft and slipped it over the obstacles. While he searched for a safer place to land, an alarm blared, warning that they were low on fuel.[2] With only seconds of fuel remaining, Neil safely lowered the hovering spacecraft to the moon's surface.

Earthlings Neil Armstrong and Buzz Aldrin had finally reached the moon!

Wearing space suits and helmets, they opened the hatch of the spacecraft. Before them was the moon, magnificent and empty. Neil climbed down a ladder and hopped to the ground. Special cameras allowed 600 million people on Earth to watch and listen.

"That's one small step for man, one giant leap for mankind," Neil said into his microphone.

Think Aloud

[2] I wonder how he feels when he hears the alarm go off. I would be afraid because it might mean I would be stuck on the moon forever!

He gathered moon rocks for scientists to study later. As he worked, his boots left marks in the dust. Neil's footprints may remain there for a million years. There is no wind, no rain, and no snow on the moon to disturb them.

Buzz climbed down the ladder and stepped onto the moon's surface.

Earth hung above them in a perfectly black sky. North Africa could be seen behind swirling white clouds.[3]

Neil shuffled over the powdery surface toward Buzz. The sun shone with a bright white light.

They were walking on the moon!

Neil stood next to Buzz. Their helmets almost touched. Buzz grinned broadly. Neil clasped his hand on his partner's shoulder.

"Isn't it *fun!*" Neil said.

On July 20, 1969, Neil Armstrong stepped on the moon and became a hero to millions of people.

But inside him was the memory of an ordinary boy from Wapakoneta, Ohio.

A boy who loved books and music.

A boy who was shy and made friends carefully.

A boy who dreamed of hanging in the air suspended only by a trapped breath.

Think Aloud

[3]*It's funny to think that we can look at the moon in the same way as they were looking at us on Earth.*

After Reading

Retell: Have children list two facts they learned about Neil Armstrong while listening to the selection.

Student Think Aloud

Use Copying Master number 7 to prompt children to summarize the beginning, middle, and end of the biography.

"This story was mostly about . . ."

Cultural Perspective

Yuri Gagarin was the first human to travel into space. The Russian cosmonaut, or astronaut, traveled around Earth in a spaceship in 1961.

Think and Respond

1. How do you think Neil Armstrong felt when he finally walked on the moon? Why? *Possible response: happy and excited because it was something he had wanted to do for a long time, and it was never done before.* **Inferential**

2. How is this biography different from a fable? *Possible responses: It contains facts and is not make-believe. It is a story about a real person.* **Genre**

3. Why did Don Brown write this story? *Possible response: He wanted to give information about Neil Armstrong to the readers.* **Author's Purpose**

SPACE FOOD

from NASA Web site

Genre: Nonfiction

Comprehension Strategy: Text Structure

Think-Aloud Copying Master number 5

Before Reading

Genre: Remind children that while biographies tell about people, other nonfiction selections give facts about things, as this one does. Invite children to recall nonfiction stories they have heard, such as "Seeds" and "The Sound of Music."

Expand Vocabulary: Introduce these words before you begin reading:

spoiling: becoming rotten

menus: lists of food choices

tortillas: very thin pancakes made of cornmeal or flour

Set a Purpose for Reading: Ask children to listen to discover what kinds of foods astronauts in outer space eat.

During Reading

Use the Think Alouds during the first reading of the story. Notes about the genre and cultural perspective may be used during subsequent readings.

Space Food

from NASA Web site

What if you went camping for six months? You would be sure to take lots of food. You would also take what you need to cook and eat it. You have to keep your food from spoiling. What would you need when you're finished eating? You would need a trash bag.

These are the kinds of things astronauts need in space.[1] There are different ways to cook space food. Some food can be eaten right away. Fruit and brownies can. Other food needs water. Spaghetti and macaroni and cheese do. These foods need heat, too. There is an oven on the Space Station. But, there is no refrigerator.

How do they keep food from spoiling? Food must be put into special packages so it won't spoil.

Astronauts eat three meals a day. They have healthy foods. Astronauts can pick their menus. They taste the different foods that they can take. They pick the ones they like. Then they get a sample menu. Those foods go into space with them.

Sample Menu		
Breakfast	**Lunch**	**Dinner**
Raspberry Yogurt	Beef Jerky	Spicy Chicken & Vegetables
Sausage Patty	Grilled Pork Chop	Potatoes au Gratin
Picante Sauce	Macaroni & Cheese	Fruit Cocktail
Tortilla	Tortilla	Dried Apricots
Oatmeal & Raisins	Almonds	Macadamia Nuts
Granola Bar	Trail Mix	Granola Bar
Orange-Pineapple Drink	Cherry-Blueberry Cobbler	Orange-Mango Drink
Coffee	Candy-Coated Chocolates	
	Orange-Pineapple Drink	

They can pick the meat they want. They can choose from different drinks. Sometimes they have fresh fruit and vegetables. Don't forget dessert! It may be candy or brownies. Astronauts don't take bread. The crumbs could float away. They would make a mess! They use <u>tortillas</u> instead.

What would happen if astronauts shook salt and pepper on their food? It would float away! It could get in their eyes. It could get into the computers.[2] And, it might make them sneeze.

So what do they do? They squirt salt and pepper out of a bottle. The salt is mixed with water. The pepper is in oil. They can add salt and pepper without it floating. Astronauts have things like ketchup, mustard and sauces in little packets.

Who cleans up when they are finished? Astronauts must throw their trash away. They don't want to be hit by a floating piece of candy.[3]

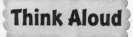

Think Aloud

[2] I never thought about small things like salt and pepper floating in space. I can see how this might hurt the computers. Salt could get stuck in the computer's buttons.

Think Aloud

[3] I think it would be funny to see candy and other food floating in space! They must have special food trays to hold the food on the plate while they are eating.

After Reading

Retell: Have children list the astronaut foods that they would most like to eat if they were in outer space.

Student Think Aloud

Use Copying Master number 5 to prompt children to tell about something they noticed the author did that helped them better understand the selection.

"I noticed that the author . . ."

Cultural Perspective

Astronauts can choose food that is popular in different parts of the world, like beef goulash, sweet and sour chicken, and Mexican scrambled eggs.

Think and Respond

1. Why would bread crumbs float around in space and not here on Earth? *Possible response: There is less gravity in space. Gravity is the force that pulls things to the ground. Without it, things float in the air.* **Inferential**

2. The author asks questions and then provides the answers. How does this help you understand the information better? *Possible responses: The author asks questions that I might ask myself. I can then listen to find out the answers.* **Genre**

3. Name one thing that the author wants you to know about space food. *Possible response: It comes in special packages.* **Author's Purpose**

DAYTIME BEDTIMES

by Cynthia J. Breedlove

Genre: Nonfiction

Comprehension Strategy: Draw Inferences

Think-Aloud Copying Master number 4

Before Reading

Genre: Remind children that nonfiction sections use facts to explain or tell about things. Invite children to think about what they learned from nonfiction selections, such as "The Sound of Music" and "I'm Growing Up!"

Expand Vocabulary: Before reading, introduce these terms:

> *shift:* a period of time
>
> *incentive:* a reason, an encouragement
>
> *restock:* put more items out for people to buy

Set a Purpose for Reading: Ask children to listen to this selection to find out what kinds of places are open twenty-four hours a day and need workers around the clock.

During Reading

Use the Think Alouds during the first reading of the story. The genre note may be used during subsequent readings.

DAYTIME BEDTIMES

by Cynthia J. Breedlove

"Go to bed; it's getting late. You need your rest for school tomorrow. Good night. It's bedtime now."

You may have heard one or all of those statements from your parents. You do need a good night of sleep to keep yourself healthy and fit. But when you become an adult, you may not be sleeping at night. You may be working.

There are human "night creatures," people who have chosen to work during the night and sleep during the day.[1] Perhaps you have a parent who works the night shift. Why would someone choose to work when most of the world is sleeping and have to try to sleep when it's light, and everybody else is up and being noisy?

Many night jobs pay more. Making more money would be an incentive to work nights. Some families have one parent who works days, and one parent who works nights so that the children always have someone home with them. Some people just like being awake all night!

What kinds of jobs are available at night? Hospitals need doctors and nurses to take care of patients at night. Many grocery stores are open 24 hours. They use the night hours to restock shelves. You may know of other stores where you live that are open 24 hours, a drugstore or a supermarket. Some factories have three different shifts: a day, an evening, and a night shift. They are busy 24 hours, too.

Airports, hotels, and some restaurants are always open. The postal service has people working through the night getting mail sorted and sent out. Office buildings get cleaned at night. Police and security guards work through the night.[2]

Are you never sleepy when it's your bedtime? Do you think that you're a night creature? Then one of these all-night jobs will be just right for you some day! (Oops, I mean, night!)

After Reading

Retell: Have children list one or two places they've learned that need nighttime workers.

Student Think Aloud

Use Copying Master number 4 to prompt children to share something they discovered while listening to the selection.

"I figured out _____ because..."

Think and Respond

1. Pretend you are a night worker. What would you be and why? *Responses will vary. Possible response: I would be a police officer, to keep everyone safe while they are sleeping.* **Analytical**

2. How does the author use questions to explain things? *Possible responses: She asks questions and then answers them. She asks the reader questions to help them understand night workers.* **Genre**

3. Why do you think Cynthia J. Breedlove wrote this article? *Possible response: She wanted readers to be aware that some people are working when most people are sleeping.* **Author's Purpose**

Dream Jobs

by John DiConsiglo

Genre: Nonfiction

Comprehension Strategy: Generate Questions

Think-Aloud Copying Master number 1

Before Reading

Genre: Remind children that nonfiction selections give us true facts about a subject. Ask them to recall what they learned about the different kinds of night workers in the nonfiction selection "Daytime Bedtimes." Then tell them that you are going to read aloud another nonfiction piece about different types of jobs.

Expand Vocabulary: Introduce these words before you read the story:

molecules: small units that make up substances like water

passion: love, a desire to do something

mascot: a person, animal, or thing that is supposed to bring good luck to a sports team

ironworkers: people who make things out of iron, such as iron beams for buildings

Set a Purpose for Reading: As you read, have children listen for things that they would like and dislike about each dream job.

During Reading

Use the Think Alouds during the first reading of the story. Notes about the genre and cultural perspective may be used during subsequent readings.

Dream Jobs

by John DiConsiglo

The butcher, the baker, and the candlestick-maker aren't the only workers out there. Here are some cool jobs you might not have heard of. With imagination and hard work, you can find *your* dream job, too!

The Bubbleologist

Bubbles aren't just for your little brother and sister anymore. Believe it or not, there's a career in playing with soap and water! Just ask Casey Carle, bubbleologist. He performs bubble tricks for everyone from school kids to cruise-ship passengers. He can balance a flaming bubble on his tongue, or wrap a person inside a giant bubble.[1] Part clown and part scientist, Casey trained with Ringling Brothers Circus to perfect his act and had to learn a lot of science. His bubbles work because he knows how to handle water <u>molecules</u>. "You need <u>passion</u> and patience to be a bubbleologist," Casey says. And his hands don't get dirty. "It's a clean job," he says.

The Insect Eater

If you're going to dinner at Florence Dunkel's house, bring a strong stomach. Florence is an entomologist—a scientist who studies bugs. But she also eats them! A typical meal might be a grasshopper stir-fry with a termite salad and roasted crickets. Insects are eaten around the world, often when food supplies are short. Most are full of vitamins and minerals. "If people got over the 'yuck' factor, they'd learn to love insects," Florence says.[2] She hopes to solve food shortages by teaching the world not to be bugged out by bugs. "Insects are the food of the future," she says. "They are delicious."

Genre Study

Nonfiction: The author lists information in some nonfiction texts. In "Dream Jobs," the author lists different types of jobs and then gives information about actual people who have these jobs.

Think Aloud

[1] *I wonder how Casey can place a flaming bubble on his tongue. How can he do that without getting burned?*

Think Aloud

[2] *I can understand what getting over the "yuck factor" means. It must mean being able to look at the bug as a meal without scrunching up your face and saying "YUCK!"*

The Mascot

When Bradley Lowe gets dressed for work, he doesn't put on a tie. He wears a 25-pound foam-and-fur costume, with Size-22 shoes and a giant feathered head. Bradley is the Bird, the Baltimore Orioles' <u>mascot</u>. As fans root, root for the home team, Bradley dances on the dugout and clowns with kids. Bradley first played a mascot in college. He went to mascot-training camp and learned gymnastics for this physically tough job. In one summer afternoon, he can sweat off 10 pounds inside his costume. But he always has a smile on his, um, beak. "I go home every night, take off my bird-head, and say, 'I had a blast at work today,'" he says.

The Alligator Wrangler

Todd Hardwick is in the pest-control business. But he doesn't fight cockroaches. He's a licensed alligator trapper.[3] Todd works in Florida, home to more than a million alligators. Most aren't dangerous, and they're naturally afraid of humans. But no one wants a stray alligator in the swimming pool. Todd usually snags a runaway gator with a rope. He ties its head and tail together. Then he tapes its mouth shut. It's dangerous, but it doesn't hurt the animal. Todd's goal is to get the gator back to the swamp alive. "I really admire alligators," he says.

The Skywalkers

It's easy to see how they got their name. <u>Ironworkers</u> like Mike Swamp and his son, Owen, seem to walk on clouds as they help build some of the world's tallest skyscrapers and bridges. Owen and Mike are Mohawk Indians, and skywalking is part of their heritage. "Mohawks get scared like everybody else," Mike says. "We just don't show it until the job is done."

Think Aloud

[3]Catching alligators? I think this "dream job" would be too dangerous for me!

After Reading

Retell: Invite children to role-play the people who have the dream jobs in this article. Children can choose a person, introduce themselves, and then explain what they do for a living using the information from the selection.

Student Think Aloud

Use Copying Master number 1 to prompt children to share questions they have about each dream job.

"I wonder . . ."

Cultural Perspective

Grasshoppers are eaten by people in Japan, Korea, and Southeast Asia. They provide protein to the people who eat them.

Think and Respond

1. Which one of these "dream jobs" would you most like to have? Why? *Responses will vary. Possible response: I would like to be a mascot. I think it would be fun to clown around at games.* **Analytical**

2. Many nonfiction selections have quotations, as this one does. Why are quotations useful in nonfiction? *Possible response: Quotations can help make a topic easier to understand and more interesting to read about.* **Genre**

3. Why do you think the author wrote this article? *Possible response: to give information about jobs that people might be interested in trying.* **Author's Purpose**

Zoo Baby Boom

by Laura Linn

Genre: Nonfiction

Comprehension Strategy: Summarize

Think-Aloud Copying Master number 7

Before Reading

Genre: Remind children that nonfiction selections give us facts about something. Invite them to recall nonfiction selections they have heard, such as "Daytime Bedtimes" and "Dream Jobs."

Expand Vocabulary: Introduce these words before you begin reading:

> *baby boom:* when more babies are born than usual
>
> *species:* a group of animals or plants that are alike in certain ways
>
> *conservation groups:* groups of people who have a common goal to protect animals or the environment
>
> *preserve:* keep safe

Set a Purpose for Reading: Ask children to listen to this story to find out how zoos can help protect endangered species, animals that are in danger of disappearing forever.

During Reading

Use the Think Alouds during the first reading of the story. Notes about the genre and cultural perspective may be used during subsequent readings.

Zoo Baby Boom

by Laura Linn

The Smithsonian National Zoo in Washington, D.C., has been hit with a <u>baby boom</u>. Three babies—a Sumatran tiger, an Asian elephant, and a western lowland gorilla—could help ensure the future of endangered animals.

All three of the new arrivals were part of the National Zoo's <u>species</u> breeding program.

"Berani, the Sumatran tiger cub, is an important example of the zoo's species survival plan," says National Zoo curator John Seidensticker. "Every birth of a Sumatran tiger is important because the species' future is very uncertain in the wild."

Berani and the other new babies are all endangered species—plants and animals that face a high risk of extinction, or disappearing forever.[1]

According to the Red List of endangered species, 5,435 animals fall into this category. But the National Zoo and other zoos around the country are working hard to give endangered animals a chance to survive.

Four-month-old Berani lives in a darkened den at the zoo with his mother. The den is kept dark so visitors can view the tigers without their knowing they are being watched. In the wild, tiger cubs stay with their mothers for about two years. Adult tigers usually live alone.

Today, less than 500 Sumatran tigers exist in the wild and about 170 live in zoos.[2]

The biggest of the new babies at the National Zoo is Kandula, a male Asian elephant. Kandula weighed 325 pounds when he was born and began walking within minutes.

Asian elephants are at risk in the wild because people hunt the males for their ivory tusks and destroy their forests for lumber. Less than 50,000 Asian elephants exist today.

The baby male gorilla who was born in November is still without a name. He spends most of his time clinging to his mother, and she is very protective of him.

Think Aloud

[1] *I think it would be horrible if an animal species disappeared forever because people did not help it stay alive.*

Think Aloud

[2] *Knowing the number of tigers left in the world is important because it makes people stop and realize what a small number that really is.*

Western lowland gorillas are from the tropical forests of West and Central Africa. The Gorilla Foundation estimates that only 10,000 to 35,000 western lowland gorillas are left in the world.

The Sumatran tiger, Asian elephant, and western lowland gorilla babies are just a few of the thousands of animals in danger of disappearing forever. But thanks to the work of zoos and conservation groups, the animals have a fighting chance.[3]

"Zoos are part of the puzzle to preserve our animals. In a zoo setting, we can do three things—celebrate the animal, study it, and help protect it," says National Zoo director Lucy Spelman.

Think Aloud

[3]*This was mostly about how the Smithsonian National Zoo is helping to keep endangered animals from becoming extinct.*

After Reading

Retell: Have children draw a picture of one of the baby animals discussed in this story. Then have them display their picture and tell something they learned about the animal from the article.

Student Think Aloud

Use Copying Master number 7 to prompt children to summarize the article.

"This story was mostly about . . ."

Cultural Perspective

Another endangered species is the Giant Panda of China. There are as few as 1,600 pandas left in the wild. Discuss why it is important that an animal doesn't disappear forever.

Think and Respond

1. Why is it safer for some endangered animals to be born in the zoo instead of in the wild? *Possible response: In the wild, these animals can be killed by people or by other animals.* **Inferential**

2. How is this story different from a biography such as "One Giant Leap"? How is it alike? *Possible responses: The two stories are different because a biography gives information about a person's life. This story gives information about a subject, endangered species. They are the same because they give facts about real things.* **Genre**

3. Why does the author think it is important for her readers to know this information? *Possible response: People have to be aware that if they don't support zoos and other groups, endangered animals could become extinct.* **Author's Purpose**

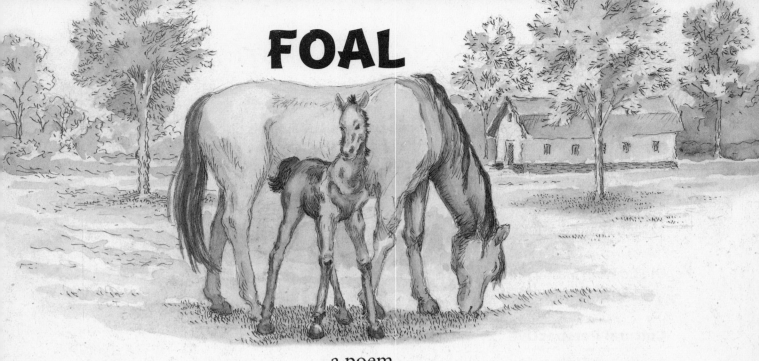

FOAL

a poem
by Mary Britton Miller

Genre: Poetry

Poetic Element: Repetition and Rhyming Words

Comprehension Strategy: Visualize

Think-Aloud Copying Master number 3

Before Reading

Genre: Remind children that poems often have rhyming words that make them pleasing to read and hear. Tell children that "Foal" is a poem that has rhyming words, but does not follow a pattern like the lines in "Hey, Bug!"

Expand Vocabulary: Before reading, introduce these terms:

whinny: a noise made by a horse

foal: a baby horse

skittish: restless

Set a Purpose for Reading: For the first reading, have children listen and enjoy the language and visualize the foal playing near its mother.

During Reading

Emphasize the rhyming words and repetition using an expressive tone. Read through the poem the first time without interruptions. Then reread, pausing to draw children's attention to the Think Aloud and genre note.

Foal

by Mary Britton Miller

Come trotting up
Beside your mother,
Little skinny.

Lay your neck across
Her back and <u>whinny</u>,
Little <u>foal</u>.

You think you're a horse
Because you can trot—
But you're not.

Your eyes are so wild,
And each leg is as tall
As a pole;[1]

And you're only a <u>skittish</u>
Child, after all,
Little foal.

Think Aloud

[1] *I am able to picture in my mind the baby horse with long, skinny legs because the author compares the legs to poles. This word paints a picture in my mind of something tall and thin.*

After Reading

Retell: Have students draw a picture of something they pictured in the poem and describe it using rhyming words.

Ask children questions to check comprehension and guide children to ask questions about the language and rhythm of the rhyme.

Student Think Aloud

Use Copying Master number 3 to prompt children to describe what they see when they think about this poem.

"I was able to picture in my mind . . ."

Think and Respond

1. How does the foal feel about its mother? *Possible response: It likes to be near her because it trots by her and lays its neck across her back.* **Inferential**

2. How is this poem like the poem "Just Watch"? *Possible responses: Certain words repeat themselves. Both of the words* foal *and* watch *are in the titles of the poems and are repeated in the poems.* **Genre**

3. How do you think the author feels about horses? *Possible responses: She likes to watch them play. She thinks of baby horses as children.* **Author's Purpose**

The Three Little Pigs

Genre: Folk Tale

Comprehension Strategy: Summarize

Think-Aloud Copying Master number 4

Before Reading

Genre: Tell children that "The Three Little Pigs" is a folk tale. Remind them that folk tales are stories that have been told and retold for many years.

Expand Vocabulary: Introduce these words before you read the story:

> *straw:* hollow stalks of plants, like wheat
>
> *cottage:* a small house
>
> *huff:* take quick, big breaths in and out
>
> *furious:* very angry

Set a Purpose for Reading: Ask children to listen to find out which little pig makes the right choice about how to build his house.

During Reading

Use the Think Alouds during the first reading of the story. The genre note and cultural perspective may be introduced during subsequent readings.

The Three Little Pigs

Once there were three little pigs who decided that the time had come for them to set off into the wide world and find homes of their own.

"Perhaps you are right, boys," said their mother. "But remember, watch out for the big, bad wolf!"

The little pigs kissed their mother and set off. Before long they became tired and sat down to rest. Just then a farmer went past, carrying a load of straw.

"With that straw I could build a strong, safe house," said the first little pig. "You two go on without me. I will stop right here."

So the first little pig said goodbye to his brothers and bought the load of straw from the farmer. He worked very hard and soon he had built the cutest little cottage you ever saw.[1]

Meanwhile, the other two little pigs had walked a good deal further when they met a woodcutter carrying a load of sticks.

"With those sticks I could build a strong, safe house," said the second little pig. "You go on without me, brother. I will stop right here."

So the second little pig said goodbye to his brother and bought the load of sticks from the woodcutter. He worked even harder than the first little pig. By suppertime, he was standing outside the cutest little house you ever saw.

Meanwhile, the third little pig had walked even further. Late that afternoon, he met a workman with a cart piled high with fine building bricks.

"With those bricks I could build a strong, safe house," said the third little pig. "I will stop right here."

So the third little pig bought the cartload of bricks from the workman and he built the neatest little brick house you ever saw.[2]

That night the first little pig slept soundly in his straw house. But at midnight there came a soft tapping on the door.

"Little pig, little pig, let me come in!" called a gruff voice.

It was the big, bad wolf! The first little pig shook with fright under the sheets but he answered bravely.

"No, no, by the hair of my chinny chin chin, I will not let you in!"

"Then I'll huff, and I'll puff, and I'll blow your house down!" shouted the wolf. And he huffed and he puffed and he blew with all his might. The house of straw blew down in a moment, but the first little pig ran as fast as he could to his brother's house of sticks.

The very next night the two little pigs were fast asleep in the house of sticks when there came a soft tapping on the door.

"Little pigs, little pigs, let me come in!" called a gruff voice.

You can guess who that was! The two little pigs trembled but they answered bravely.

"No, no, by the hair of our chinny chin chins, we will not let you in!"

"Then I'll huff, and I'll puff, and I'll blow your house down!" shouted the wolf. And he huffed and he puffed and he blew with all his might. The house of sticks blew down in a moment, but the two little pigs ran as fast as they could to their brother's house of bricks.

Another day passed and the three little pigs went to bed in the house of bricks. In the middle of the night there came a soft tapping on the door.

"Little pigs, little pigs, let me come in!" called a gruff voice.

The three little pigs knew at once who it was but they hugged each other and answered bravely.

"No, no, by the hair of our chinny chin chins, we will not let you in!"

"Then I'll huff, and I'll puff, and I'll blow your house down!" shouted the wolf. And he huffed and he puffed and he blew with all his might. But the house remained standing.

The wolf was *furious*. "If they won't let me in the door," he said to himself, "I'll climb down the chimney!"

But the third little pig heard the wolf creeping across the roof and he quickly put a huge pot of water on the fire.[3] When the wolf jumped down the chimney, he landed with a splash in the pot and was boiled to bits. And that was the end of the big, bad wolf!

Think Aloud

[3]I can figure out that the third pig is smarter than his brothers. He knows how to build a strong house and how to act quickly.

After Reading

Retell: Have children act out the story. Remind them to think about the order of events in the story before they begin.

Student Think Aloud

Use Copying Master number 4 to prompt children to share something they figured out about characters or actions in the story.

"I figured out _____ because . . ."

Cultural Perspective

The pigs in this story may not have been pigs at all. Young pigs do not have hair on their chins; young goats do. In a similar tale from Germany, the wolf visits young goats instead of pigs.

Think and Respond

1. How would this story be different if all of the little pigs had built brick houses? *Possible response: The wolf would not have been able to blow any of the houses down. The wolf probably would have left them all alone.* **Critical**

2. Identify places in this story where words and lines are repeated. *Possible responses: Little pigs, little pigs, let me come in! No, no, by the hair of our chinny chin chins, we will not let you in!* **Genre**

3. Why do you think this story has been told over and over again? *Possible responses: It states the lesson that you should take the time to do something right like the little pig who built the brick house. It is also fun to see how the third little pig outsmarts the big bad wolf.* **Author's Purpose**

LONDON BRIDGE IS FALLING DOWN

a nursery rhyme

Genre: Nursery Rhyme

Poetic Element: Repetition and Rhythm

Comprehension Strategy: Generate Questions

Think-Aloud Copying Master number 1

Before Reading

Genre: Remind children that a nursery rhyme is a short, rhyming poem for children. Explain to children that versions of this nursery rhyme have been around for hundreds of years. Some children may know this Mother Goose rhyme as a song and a game. Discuss other nursery rhymes children may have heard, such as "Mary Had a Little Lamb."

Expand Vocabulary: Introduce these words before you begin reading:

fair: nice, kind, beautiful

mortar: a mixture of cement, sand, and water used to hold bricks and stones together

Set a Purpose for Reading: Invite children to listen to this nursery rhyme to find out what materials are suggested to build London Bridge.

During Reading

Read the nursery rhyme first without interruptions, using body movements or foot-tapping to emphasize the rhyme's rhythm. Use the Think Aloud and genre note during subsequent readings.

London Bridge Is Falling Down

London Bridge is falling down,

Falling down, falling down,

London Bridge is falling down,

My <u>fair</u> lady.[1]

Build it up with wood and clay,

Wood and clay, wood and clay,

Build it up with wood and clay,

My fair lady.

Wood and clay will wash away,

Wash away, wash away,

Wood and clay will wash away,

My fair lady.

Build it up with bricks and <u>mortar</u>,

Bricks and mortar, bricks and mortar,

Build it up with bricks and mortar,

My fair lady.

Think Aloud

[1]*I wonder who "my fair lady" is. It makes me think of a princess or a queen.*

Genre Study

Nursery Rhyme:
Nursery rhymes have a certain rhythm that allows them to easily be turned into songs. This rhyme is often used in a game by the same name.

After Reading

Retell: Have children sing the poem as they perform the traditional movement activity to it.

Ask children questions to check comprehension and guide children to ask questions about the language and rhythm of the rhyme.

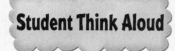
Student Think Aloud

Use Copying Master number 1 to prompt children to ask questions about this nursery rhyme.

"I wonder . . ."

Cultural Perspective

The real London Bridge was built in London, England, in 1831. Over a hundred years later it was taken apart and rebuilt in Arizona, where it still stands today. Discuss with children how the poem reflects a different culture and time period.

Think and Respond

1. Why would bricks and mortar be a better choice for building London Bridge than wood and clay? *Possible response: Bricks and mortar are more waterproof than clay.* **Inferential**

2. How is this nursery rhyme like "Mary Had a Little Lamb"? *Possible responses: They both have repeating lines. They both have a rhythm that is also a song.* **Genre**

3. Why did the author write this nursery rhyme for children? *Possible responses: It is fun to sing. It is easy to remember. They can play a game while singing this rhyme.* **Author's Purpose**

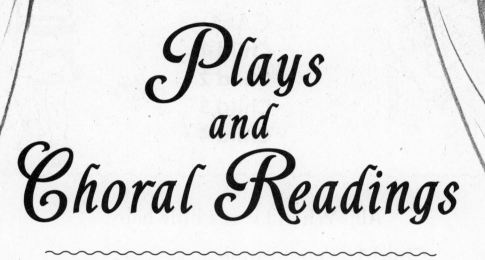

Plays and Choral Readings

Look at Me Now

by Alice Boynton

CAST:
Child 1
Child 2
Child 3
Child 4

All: When I was a little baby,

Child 1: I could smile.

Child 2: I could cry.

Child 3: I could drink milk.

Child 4: I could hold my toes.

All: But when I was a little baby,

Child 1: I couldn't eat spaghetti.

Child 2: I couldn't say my name.

Child 3: I couldn't catch a ball.

Child 4: I couldn't play games.

All: Just look at me now!

All: When I was one year old,

Child 1: I could wave.

Child 2: I could walk.

Child 3: I could play peekaboo.

Child 4: I could sit in a highchair.

All: But when I was one year old,

Child 1: I couldn't talk on the telephone,

Child 2: I couldn't draw an elephant.

Child 3: I couldn't climb a tree.

Child 4: I couldn't wash my hands.

All: Just look at me now!

All: When I was two years old,

Child 1: I could play in the sandbox.

Child 2: I could look at picture books.

Child 3: I could eat with a spoon.

Child 4: I could blow bubbles.

All: But when I was two years old,

Child 1: I couldn't write my name.

Child 2: I couldn't jump rope.

Child 3: I couldn't button my coat.

Child 4: I couldn't make a tent.

All: Just look at me now!

All: When I was three years old,

Child 1: I could ride a tricycle.

Child 2: I could count 1, 2, 3.

Child 3: I could put on my socks.

Child 4: I could build with blocks.

All: But when I was three years old,

Child 1: I couldn't read a story.

Child 2: I couldn't pour my juice.

Child 3: I couldn't tie my shoes.

Child 4: I couldn't skip.

All: Just look at me now!

All: When I was four years old,

Child 1: I could dance and sing.

Child 2: I could wash the dog.

Child 3: I could paint.

Child 4: I could brush my teeth.

All: But when I was four years old,

Child 1: I couldn't push a big cart.

Child 2: I couldn't write the letters.

Child 3: I couldn't play kickball.

Child 4: I couldn't count to fifty.

All: Just look at me now!

All: When I was five years old,

Child 1: I could stand on one foot.

Child 2: I could make my bed.

Child 3: I could play dress-up.

Child 4: I could do puzzles.

All: But when I was five years old,

Child 1: I couldn't make a sandwich.

Child 2: I couldn't spell <u>pig</u>.

Child 3: I couldn't remember my address.

Child 4: I couldn't count by tens.

All: Just look at me now!

All: Now I'm in first grade.

Child 1: I can stand on my head.

Child 2: I can be in a play.

Child 3: I can set the table.

Child 4: I can read numbers.

All: And now that I'm in first grade,

Child 1: I can fly a kite.

Child 2: I can add $3 + 2 = 5$.

Child 3: I can feed my bird.

Child 4: I can play in a band.

All: Just look at me now!

I Speak, I Say, I Talk

by Arnold L. Shapiro

Solo 1: Cats purr.

Solo 2: Lions roar.

Solo 3: Owls hoot.

Solo 4: Bears snore.

Solo 5: Crickets creak.

Solo 6: Mice squeak.

Solo 7: Sheep baa.

All: But I SPEAK!

Solo 1: Monkeys chatter.

Solo 2: Cows moo.

Solo 3: Ducks quack.

Solo 4: Doves coo.

Solo 5: Pigs squeal.

Solo 6: Horses neigh.

Solo 7: Chickens cluck.

All: But I SAY!

Solo 1: Flies hum.

Solo 2: Dogs growl.

Solo 3: Bats screech.

Solo 4: Coyotes howl.

Solo 5: Frogs croak.

Solo 6: Parrots squawk.

Solo 7: Bees buzz.

All: But I TALK!

© Macmillan/McGraw-Hill

SHADOW DANCE

by Ivy O. Eastwick

Group 1: O Shadow,
Dear Shadow,
Come, Shadow,
And dance!

Group 2: On the wall
In the firelight
Let both of
Us prance!

Solo 1: I raise my arms, thus!

Solo 2: And you raise
Your arms, so!

Group 1: And dancing
And leaping
And laughing
We go!

Group 2: From the wall
To the ceiling
From ceiling
To wall,

All: Just you and
I, Shadow,
And none else
At all.

© Macmillan/McGraw-Hill

Fooba Wooba John

American folk song

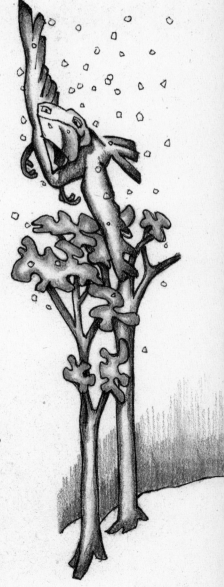

Solo 1: Saw a flea kick a tree,

All: Fooba wooba, fooba wooba,

Solo 1: Saw a flea kick a tree,

All: Fooba wooba John.

Solo 1: Saw a flea kick a tree
In the middle of the sea,

All: Fooba wooba, fooba wooba,
Fooba wooba John.

Solo 2: Saw a crow flying low,

All: Fooba wooba, fooba wooba,

Solo 2: Saw a crow flying low,

All: Fooba wooba John.

Solo 2: Saw a crow flying low
Several miles beneath the snow,

All: Fooba wooba, fooba wooba,
Fooba wooba John.

Solo 3: Saw a whale chase a snail,

All: Fooba wooba, fooba wooba,

Solo 3: Saw a whale chase a snail,

All: Fooba wooba John.

Solo 3: Saw a whale chase a snail
All around a water pail,

All: Fooba wooba, fooba wooba,
Fooba wooba John.

Solo 4: Saw a bear scratch his ear,

All: Fooba wooba, fooba wooba,

Solo 4: Saw a bear scratch his ear,

All: Fooba wooba John.

Solo 4: Saw a bear scratch his ear
Wonderin' what we're doing here,

All: Fooba wooba, fooba wooba,
Fooba wooba John.

SUPPER with the QUEEN

by Sally Jarvis

CAST:
William
Storyteller
Queen
1st Traveler
2nd Traveler

William: Here I am in the woods. What can I eat for supper?

Storyteller: He looks in his pockets.

William: Oh, ho! Here is an onion! I will have onion soup!

Storyteller: He makes a fire. He puts a pan on the fire and he puts in some water and the onion.

1st Traveler: Well, what do I see here? Are you cooking supper?

William: Yes. It is onion soup!

1st Traveler: If I help you cook it, may I have some, too?

William: That's fair. How can you help?

1st Traveler: I have a banana. There is nothing like a banana to make good soup.

William: Banana soup? I don't think . . .

Storyteller: But it is too late. The traveler has put the banana into the soup, skin and all.

2nd Traveler: Well, hello! Are you two having supper?

William: We are cooking some soup.

2nd Traveler: If I help you cook it, may I eat it with you?

1st Traveler: How will you help?

2nd Traveler: I have some good pig's feet. I will put them into the soup.

William: But . . .

Storyteller: Too late! The traveler puts the pig's feet into the soup. A queen comes into the woods.

Queen: What, ho! What are you doing in my woods?

William: Oh, dear me! We didn't know the woods were yours!

1st Traveler: We are having supper. Do you mind?

Queen: Well . . .

2nd Traveler: Would you have supper with us?

Queen: I think that would be fun! I have never eaten outside.

Storyteller: She sits down. William gives out the soup. They each take a sip.

1st Traveler: Ugh!

2nd Traveler: Ugh!

Queen: Ugh! What is in this soup?

William: There are onions, bananas, and pig's feet.

Storyteller: She is smart but she doesn't know how to cook.

Queen: No wonder it is no good. It doesn't have any chocolate cake in it. Everything tastes better with chocolate cake. How lucky I have some with me!

Storyteller: Before William can say a word, the queen drops some chocolate cake into the soup.

1st Traveler: Now some salt.

William: But . . .

2nd Traveler: Here is the pepper!

William: But . . .

Queen: Did you put in any sugar?

Storyteller: William walks away.

William: I will just go hungry. The next time there will be one cook—ME!

Cultural Perspective

Guide children to perform the play. Ask questions to check comprehension and guide children to ask questions about the characters, plot, and setting. Discuss with children that the play takes place in a different culture and time period.

That Goat Has GOT to Go!

by Anne M. Miranda

CAST:

Storyteller	**Grandma Ann**
Sister Kate	**Goat**
Cousin Steve	**Mother**
Joe	**Grandpa Pete**
Brother Bill	**Auntie Bess**
Father	

Storyteller: Young Kate and Steve and Brother Bill all live with Joe, high on a hill. A lot of pets live in their house—a dog, a cat, and one gray mouse.

Brother Bill: I have a dog that likes to run. My dog and I have lots of fun.

Sister Kate: I have a cat with yellow fur. My cat is soft and likes to purr.

Cousin Steve: I have a mouse with little feet. Hard cheese is what it likes to eat.

Joe: I have no pet to hug and squeeze—No dog, no cat, no mouse, no cheese! I think I'll get a billy goat. I'll feed him hay and brush his coat.

Storyteller: Joe got a billy goat that day. But did that goat eat nice fresh hay? Oh, no! What did he find to munch? A pair of purple socks for lunch!

Goat: Bleat, bleat! Socks to eat.

Storyteller: Goat ate and ate and did not rest. The family said he was a pest.

Mother: I had a juicy peach, you see. But that goat ate it—one, two, three!

Goat: Bleat, bleat! Peach to eat.

Mother: No peach for Mother? Listen, Joe, I think that goat has got to go.

Father: I had two shoes, a left and right. But that goat ate them both one night.

Goat: Bleat, bleat! Shoes to eat.

Father: No shoes for Father? Listen, Joe, I think that goat has got to go!

Sister Kate: I put some fish on my cat's plate. The kitty's fish is what Goat ate.

Goat: Bleat, bleat! Fish to eat.

Sister Kate: No fish for kitty? Listen, Joe, I think that goat has got to go!

Brother Bill: I had a favorite baseball mitt. That goat of Joe's ate every bit.

Goat: Bleat, bleat! Mitt to eat.

Brother Bill: No mitt for baseball? Listen, Joe, I think that goat has got to go!

Grandpa Pete: I hung my clothes outside to dry. Goat ate my sweater, belt, and tie.

Goat: Bleat, bleat! Clothes to eat.

Grandpa Pete: No clothes for Grandpa? Listen, Joe, I think that goat has got to go!

Grandma Ann: I set a pie out on the sill. That goat sat down and ate his fill.

Goat: Bleat, bleat! Pie to eat.

Grandma Ann: No pie for supper? Listen, Joe, I think that goat has got to go!

Auntie Bess: I had a yellow hat with bows. Why that goat ate it, goodness knows!

Goat: Bleat, bleat! Hat to eat.

Auntie Bess: No hat for Auntie? Listen, Joe, I think that goat has got to go!

Cousin Steve: I put my coat down on a chair. When I came back it wasn't there!

Goat: Bleat, bleat! Coat to eat.

Cousin Steve: No coat for winter? Listen, Joe, I think that goat has got to go!

Joe: Oh, I am feeling sad and blue. My goat has eaten Father's shoe. He ate a mitt, a hat, and tie. He ate my grandma's apple pie. What can I do to stop my goat from eating Steve's warm winter coat? I'll have to tie him with a rope. Then he can't be a pest, I hope.

Storyteller: Joe walked to school one foggy day. He didn't stop to laugh or play. Joe and his goat marched down the trail. He had his lunch inside a pail. An apple fell out on the ground. A sandwich dropped without a sound. Some carrot sticks were next to go. Soon there was no lunch left for Joe. At school, Joe told his pet to wait. He tied Goat to the big front gate. Joe went to class. And then at noon he got his lunch pail, fork, and spoon.

© Macmillan/McGraw-Hill

Storyteller: There was no lunch inside Joe's pail. He lost his food along the trail. Each thing had fallen bit by bit. But Joe thought Goat had eaten it.

Joe: No food at lunch time? That's not nice! I should have gotten two pet mice. No dog would eat my lunch like that. And neither would a kitty cat.

Goat: Bleat, bleat! Nothing to eat.

Storyteller: Soon it was time for Joe to go. But thick fog made the going slow. Joe could not see one step ahead. He held Goat's rope and shook his head.

Joe: I think that we are lost, my friend. I cannot see around the bend. I cannot see a tree or log. I cannot see in all this fog.

Storyteller: Just then, that goat began to bleat! His nose found something good to eat.

Goat: Bleat, bleat! Meat to eat!

Joe: I'll stop and let you look around. Please, tell me, what else have you found?

Goat: Bleat, bleat! Bread to eat.

Joe: You found my sandwich on the trail! It must have fallen from my pail.

Goat: Bleat, bleat! Apple to eat.

Joe: Just find what's next along the trail. Please find what's missing from my pail. That's how we'll get back home today. Your nose will help us find the way.

Storyteller: Back home, his Mom and Dad and Bill all looked for Joe up on the hill. His Grandma Ann beat on a pail. And Grandpa yelled along the trail.

Joe: Yoo-hoo! I'm here! I'm safe and sound. Thanks to my goat and what he found.

Storyteller: Then everybody jumped for joy. They saw that goat and their lost boy.

Joe: My goat has led me to my house. He's better than a little mouse. He's better than a cat or dog. He led me home in this thick fog. Please tell me, does Goat have to go? Both he and I just have to know!

All : That goat's a hero! Hip hooray! We think that goat has got to stay!

Storyteller: Sister Kate and Joe's big brother, Auntie Bess and Dad and Mother, his Grandma, Steve, and Grandpa Pete all gave that goat a great big treat.

Mother: Have a peach!

Grandma Ann: Try some pie!

Sister Kate: Want some fish?

Grandpa Pete : Eat my tie!

Brother Bill : Here's a baseball!

Father: Chew my slipper!

Auntie Bess: Taste my hat?

Cousin Steve: Try this zipper.

Goat: Bleat, bleat! Treats to eat!

All: That goat's a hero! Hip hooray! Yes, yes! That goat has got to stay!

Think-Aloud
COPYING MASTERS

I wonder . . .

I made a connection when . . .

I figured out _____ because . . .

Think-Aloud Copying Master 5

I thought _____ was important in this text because . . .

When I read _____,
I had to re-read,
read back, read on . . .

LITERATURE INDEX by GENRE

Biography

Fiction

Folk Tales, Tall Tales, and Fables

Nonfiction

Plays and Choral Readings

Poetry

Songs

ACKNOWLEDGMENTS —————————— Continued

ACKNOWLEDGMENTS ⁓⁓⁓⁓⁓⁓⁓⁓ Continued

ACKNOWLEDGMENTS ───────── Continued

"Supper with the Queen" by Sally Jarvis. Copyright © 1965 by Parents' Magazine Press, a division of Parents' Magazine Enterprises, Inc. Used by permission of Parents' Magazine Enterprises, Inc.

"Close Friends" by Sally Lucas from HIGHLIGHTS FOR CHILDREN, Jan. 1997, Vol. 52, Issue 1. Copyright © 1997 for Highlights for Children. Used by permission of Highlights for Children.

Cover Illustrations: Valerie Sokolova

Illustrators Credits: Neecy Twinem, 9–13, 133–136, 230–233; Kathy Wilburn, 14–18, 93–95; Ruth Flanigan, 9–21, 110–114, 156–159, 257–260; Kelly Murphy, 22–25; Jan Naimo Jones, 26–27; Carol Koeller, 28–31, 75–77, 191–195; Nicole in den Bosch, 32–34, 62–65, 146–148; Tatjana Mai-Wyss, 35–37, 149–152; Carol Schwartz, 38–42, 196–198; Amanda Harvey, 43–47; Hector Borlasca, 48–52, 107–109, 261–267; Susan Spellman, 53–57, 130–132; Ka Botzis, 58–61, 177–181; Marika Hahn, 66–71, 143–145; Eva Cockrille, 72–74, 246–250; Sandy Rabinowitz, 78–81; Paula Wendland, 87–89, 210–212; Valerie Sokolova, 90–92, 251–252; Paige Billin-Frye, 96–98; Donald Cook, 104–106, 234–236; Doug Panton, 115–119; Kathleen Kemly, 120–123; Janet Montecalvo, 124–129, 207–209; Madeline Sorel, 137–139; Ashley Mims, 140–142; Laurie Harden, 153–155, 219–222; Kate Flanagan, 160–162, 188–190; Margeaux Lucas, 163–168; Bridget Starr Taylor, 169–173; Gioia Fiammenghi, 174–176; Nancy Lane, 182–184; Erin Eitter Kono, 185–187; Marcy Ramsey, 199–206; Stephen Marchesi, 213–218; Barbara Pollack, 223–225; Brian Lies, 226–229; Gerry O'Neill, 237–240; Ana Larranaga, 241–243; Brian Langdo, 253–254; Terri Murphy, 255–256